T0274076

THE FLETCHER JONES FOUNDATION
HUMANITIES IMPRINT

The Fletcher Jones Foundation has endowed this imprint to foster innovative and enduring scholarship in the humanities.

The publisher and the University of California Press Foundation gratefully acknowledge the generous support of the Fletcher Jones Foundation Imprint in Humanities.

In Praise of Polytheism

In Praise of Polytheism

Maurizio Bettini

Translated from the Italian

UNIVERSITY OF CALIFORNIA PRESS

University of California Press
Oakland, California

© 2014 by Società editrice il Mulino, Bologna

Library of Congress Cataloging-in-Publication Data

ISBN 978-0-520-34224-8 (cloth : alk. paper)
ISBN 978-0-520-97458-6 (ebook)

Manufactured in the United States of America

28 27 26 25 24 23 22
10 9 8 7 6 5 4 3 2 1

CONTENTS

Introduction

The Gods in Exile

It's fairly uncommon to page through a book of philosophy without coming across at least one quotation by Plato. This is true not only for academic or scholarly works dedicated to ancient philosophy, but for philosophical writings in general. Philosophers are always conversing with Plato. In the same way, people interested in semiotics read Aristotle, alongside the works of Charles S. Pierce, and St. Augustine too. And even popular books about democracy (a critical topic these days), often find inspiration, for better or for worse, in the Greek forms of democracy, especially the one from Athens. I mention these facts in order to defend a rather obvious thesis: classical antiquity is not just a popular topic for professional classicists or students working their way through the *consecutio temporum;* it constitutes a source of inspiration, a living source, for contemporary cultural production.

This is clearly true in other fields spanning across literature (from Seamus Heaney to Derek Walcott), the visual arts (the numerous ancient works "re-envisioned" by contemporary artists), theater (new productions of Greek tragedies are often genuine rewritings), up to the tenth muse of cinema. Even though the ancients will never know anything about it, they have been for the moderns the muses for whom they searched. I can safely claim that just as happened in the past—in the Middle Ages, in the Renaissance, and in the Age of Enlightenment or in the 1900s—Greek and Roman cultural creations remain relevant, and continue to provide food for thought for today's culture. It is not my intention here to discuss how and to what extent this classical presence is still alive in the contemporary world, and even less to compare our times to those of the past. This is not my aim. I simply want to highlight how classical philosophy, politics, literature, art, and theater (that is, the vast majority of their cultural production) stay relevant not only as objects of study for Greek and Roman scholars, but how they interact daily with contemporary culture. And religion? Can we say the same about the many religions of classical antiquity? Do they play a similar role today?

These questions may sound bizarre, since according to conventional wisdom, religion is not considered a form of cultural production comparable to theater or art. Religion gives the impression of being "something else." We really should know better, though, when we are discussing civilizations—especially the ancient ones—in which sculpture was intended to provide religious imagery, poetry was often construed as an offering to the gods on a par with material sacrifice, rituals were regularly accompanied by music and song, and ceremonies were carried out in buildings whose architecture is still admired today. And this doesn't even begin to take into consideration that a large part of what we call classical literature could be categorized as stories about gods and heroes, and thus—from a certain point of view—as works of a "religious" character. There is no question, therefore, that religion in the ancient world was a legitimate cultural product; moreover, it was a locus in which multiple cultural forms were interlaced. The fact that religion is a fully cultural construct is fairly evident: if it weren't, its practices and organization would not have changed so radically from one era to another, from one continent to another, or from one nation to another. Why, then, does ancient religion remain tightly closed behind the doors of university departments (those few in which it is still taught, incidentally) and provide material for scholarly conferences, yet never seems to interact with contemporary culture to the same degree as theater or philosophy?

The answer is predictable enough: because Christianity has, since its beginnings, gradually positioned itself *against* ancient religions, relegating them to the territory of falsehood and error. And Christianity is not only still alive and well, compared to the ancient religions, but it has earned a place as the dominant religion in many parts of the globe. More importantly, it even influences a large portion of the cultural perceptions of people who are no longer or have never been Christians, but who are nevertheless part of a post-Christian civilization. Although it is not explicitly stated anymore (and for obvious reasons, since the ancient gods lost their followers quite a long time ago), the original Christian censure remains present in the very words that are used to define the Greek and Roman religions: words such as "paganism," "idolatry," and "polytheism" itself (about which we will speak later).[1] But in addition to this, in popular credence, ancient religion is seen as an *obsolete* religion, defeated by the advance of civilization as much as by Christianity itself. This idea, according to the evolutionary vision of religious phenomena, has been upheld not only by Christian theologians or philosophers, but also by past generations of historians of religion. But there's one problem with this reconstruction, one that makes it rather difficult to accept this version of the facts: to claim that Greek or Roman religion is obsolete is no different from declaring that the poems of Homer or Virgil are obsolete. This argument could have meant something during the period of the "querelle des anciens et des modernes," but it would lose any such relevance today. We have long understood that cultural products cannot be judged on the scale of time or evolution, and this is equally true for religion. We are now well aware of the degree of colonialist and Eurocentric thought hiding under the cloak of certain evolutionary hierarchies. The Greek or Roman religion is simply *another* religion, or better yet, *a* religion, just like Shinto or Islam. And yet it is not ordinarily seen as such.[2]

If we return to the theme of Christian censure, we see that whenever any aspect of the Greek or Roman religion managed to escape this censorship, it was only because it had changed its meaning or its identity. The gods who were honored and venerated by two civilizations, and who were at the center of quite complex social, cultural, and intellectual organizations, have been shrunk down, transformed into characters from a generic "mythology," turned into mere actors within tales of fantasy. The results of this metamorphosis, carried out centuries ago, are still very much present in our culture. To take one example, the Wikipedia page about the goddess Juno is entitled "Juno (mythology)." Already in the early 1800s, the Italian poet Giacomo Leopardi had understood how pointless any appeal to classical "mythology" was "since we haven't inherited the Greek and Latin religion like we have their literature."[3] In a similar manner, ancient religious statues have been downgraded into generic works of art, an Aphrodite or a Dionysus whose beauty we contemplate and whose sculptors we admire without considering that these images were representations of divinities, not of characters in a "myth." All the rest, the entire complex system of relationships that tied people and gods to each other in the Greek and Roman world, has taken on the position of an academic subject—though in truth, this was a hard-earned status that only became completely autonomous in the early nineteenth century.[4] In conclusion, we can agree with Heine that the ancient gods have indeed been "exiled," although not into "the obscurity of dismantled temples or in enchanted groves,"[5] as the German poet evocatively put it, but into universities and research institutes. This has happened to such an extent that, as far as we can tell, they have little chance to be reincarnated these days, contrary to what happened once upon a time to Dionysus/Denys l'Auxerrois and Apollo/Duke Carl von Rosenmold in Walter Pater's "imaginary portraits".[6]

Although the movie industry has revived many ancient gods, hybridizing them with Marvel characters, ancient polytheism (from this point forward I too will call it by this name) is not a source of living inspiration for modern and contemporary culture comparable to the Greek and Roman philosophy and theater. I do not mean to suggest that there have not been modern poets, philosophers, writers, or directors who celebrated the values of polytheism. But this is not the place to investigate the history of such a complex phenomenon.[7] It is worth mentioning, though, that when we look more closely at the method and the perspective with which some of the most famous apologists of the ancient gods approached the subject, we notice that theirs was a mostly metaphorical polytheism: an enchanting *medium* brought into use to represent something that had very little to do with the real practice of ancient religion.[8] In a letter to Max Jacobi, for example, Goethe declared that he felt "polytheist" as an artist (just as he felt "pantheist" as a scientist and "Christian" in terms of his morality). Goethe professed an artistic polytheism that, moreover, fell in line with the declarations contained in the mysterious "Program of German Idealism" found amongst Hegel's papers and written (or transcribed) in his handwriting:

> Poetry thereby obtains a higher dignity [...]. At the same time we so often hear that the great multitude should have a sensual religion. Not only the great multitude, but even philosophy needs it. *Monotheism of reason and the heart, polytheism of the imagination and art, that is what we need!* [...] we must have a new mythology; this mythology must, however, stand in the service of ideas, it must become a mythology of reason. Until we make ideas aesthetic, i.e. mythological, they hold no interest for the people, and conversely, before mythology is reasonable, the philosopher must be ashamed of it.[9]

The "sensual religion" to which this programmatic "polytheism of the imagination and art" should provide nourishment is—in no uncertain terms—nothing other than poetry. Friedrich Nietzsche, in his anti-Christian polemics, makes an appeal to polytheism as a preparatory step toward the birth of individualism. "One god," he wrote, "was not considered a denial of another god, nor blasphemy against him. It was here that the luxury of individuals was first permitted; it was here that one first honored the rights of individuals. The invention of gods, heroes, and overmen of all kinds [...] was the inestimable preliminary exercise for the justification of the egoism and sovereignty of the individual."[10] Polytheism was the earliest origins of morality, in the Nietzschean sense, obviously.

During the 1900s, though, polytheism would begin to enjoy an important vibrancy as the representation (or rather, once again, as the metaphor) of psychological traits. Carl Gustav Jung wrote:

> But the things we have outgrown are only the word-ghosts, *not the psychic facts which were responsible for the birth of the gods.* We are just as

much possessed by our autonomous psychic contents as if they were gods. Today they are called phobias, compulsions, etc., or briefly, neurotic symptoms. The gods have become diseases; not Zeus, but the solar plexus, now rules Olympus.[11]

The psychological project of James Hillman takes direct inspiration from Jung's assertions (though perhaps not from their irony) when it makes an attempt to recognize

the Gods as themselves pathologized, the 'infirmitas of the archetype.' Without elaborating what is familiar to you, I think the main point is made if we recognize that Greek myths ... require the odd, peculiar, extreme—the Abnormal Psychology of the Gods.[12]

And even without bringing in the subject of archetypes, Mallarmé had already recognized that "if the gods don't do anything discreditable, then they are no longer gods."[13] At least Ezra Pound, who was in his own way an apologist for psychological polytheism, explicitly acknowledged the metaphorical quality of this return to the ancient gods. Perhaps because his *Guide to Kulchur* had not been written

for the over-fed. It is written for men who have not been able to afford a university education or for young men, whether or not threatened with universities, who want to know more at the age of fifty than I know today [...].[14]

The Bard of Idaho, as he was called by Ford Madox Ford, would also write the following:

Eleusis did not distort truth by exaggerating the individual, neither could it have violated the individual spirit. Only in the high air and the great clarity can there be a just estimation of values. [...] *No apter metaphor having been found for certain emotional colors, I assert that the Gods exist.* [...] I assert that a great treasure of verity exists for all

> mankind in Ovid and in the subject matter of Ovid's long poem, and that only in this form could it be registered.[15]

In a different manner, polytheism would also work as an aesthetic metaphor for philosophers or poets, as a different perspective for viewing the world. This is what happens in the absorbing pages that Fernando Pessoa, under the heteronym of Antonio Mora (in his introduction to the even more unreal Alberto Caeiro), dedicated to *The Return of the Gods*, laying out a resolutely heated debate against "Christ-ism," particularly in its Iberian version. The "paganism" that Pessoa/Mora preached had at its center an enigmatic verse by Caeiro, which Mora believed to be even more "pagan" that any pagan himself would have been able to write: "Nature is parts without a whole."[16]

The much more recent essay by Odo Marquard, "In Praise of Polytheism," in spite of its title, is more in praise of mythology than of ancient religion. Or perhaps it is better to call it an apology for the *pluralism* that can be found in tales of classical mythology, presented as examples of how "polymythical" thought can provide multiple solutions to experiences. This is in contrast to "monomythical" thought, defined as such because it is tied to a single unique tale, which is what characterizes monotheism.[17] Compared to Marquard's thinking, made fragile by yet another conflation between polytheism and mythology, I certainly prefer the following sentence from Antonio Tabucchi: "Doubt, like literature, is polytheist."[18]

Perhaps it is only William James, as Amos Funkenstein pointed out, who turned to ancient polytheism in order to ask for something that offered a true immediacy towards life, to the concrete experience of people, and not for aesthetics or psychology.[19] In his pragmatism, in fact, James evaluated the polytheist hypothesis in terms of what it could *mean* for an individual: "cash-value," the formula that was so crucial for him, and that he used even in his reflections on religion. As James reiterated many times, "the cash-value of any concept [...] was in how the concept helped the individual to cope, how it aided the individual in his or her actual, practical, and concrete experiences."[20] It is for this very reason, for the pragmatic, human, vital orientation that James brought to his thoughts about religion and to polytheism in general, that I too would like to borrow his concept: the cash-value of polytheism is definitively at the center of my work.

The reflections that follow will explore what ancient polytheism, and in particular Roman polytheism, could offer our society today, not in terms of aesthetics or philosophy, literature or psychology, but in terms of concrete experience, both individual and collective, simultaneously political and social. This is the principle that has both guided me through my studies and represented their purpose: bringing to light the *repressed potential* of polytheism, providing a space in which its way of constructing a relationship with the divine could furnish answers to some of the problems for which monotheistic religions—as we know them in and through the Western world—cannot find a solution, or which are created directly by monotheism itself. Taking examples that come mostly from the Roman religion, I have thus chosen to focus on the aspects of polytheism that, if they were assimilated by our societies, could help alleviate one of the many evils that continues to afflict us: *religious conflict,* and alongside this, that variegated specter of hostility, blame, and indifference that still today blinds "our" eyes toward "their" gods. But before setting out on this long voyage, I must pause for a brief clarification.

By favoring the specifically sociopolitical cash-value that ancient religions could provide to contemporary life, I certainly do not wish to ignore the other values, of a more intellectual character, that they could equally offer to my reflections—in particular, their ability to formulate the human experience by identifying and intermixing concepts, images, and actions in quite unexpected manners. Let's try to picture in our minds, just for a moment, a culture in which a child's life corresponds to a series of steps, each one accompanied by a god. Lucina brings children into the light, Vitumnus and Sentinus give them life and emotions, Vaticanus opens their mouths for their first cry, Levana lifts them from the ground, Cunina rocks them, Potina and Educa give them drink and food, Farinus gives them their first meaningful word, and so on—up to the two goddesses who will take care of them the moment they leave home: Iterduca in their going away, Domiduca to ensure their return. We are witnessing a sequence of "minuscule" gods, as the Romans called them, who not only oversee specific actions, but *represent* them as religious agents: divinities who function simultaneously as ways of doing and as cognitive categories. What I have just written here, though, constitutes only half of the intellectual process put into motion by the Roman religion in its representation and structuring of reality. If it tends to *subdivide* experience into a sequence of divine agents, it equally veers off in the opposite direction: *grouping them together* according to specific elements that for us would be considered absolutely disparate, under the name of a single god. Mars, for example, whom we all know as the god of war, can also be invoked to ensure a successful harvest or the well-being of animal stock. At first glance, these different attributions throw us off: why should we mix war, the fertility of the fields, and the health of oxen all together? Because these moments have as their common denominator a single feature: danger. The dangers of war when you enter the battlefield, the dangers arising from natural calamities when the crops are growing, the dangers in the woods when the animals are out to pasture. This explains why in each of these cases the same god is called upon for intervention: warlike Mars. Going back in time to tease out this ancient web, cutting and reconstructing reality according to the guidelines indicated by classical religions, offers a precious incentive to anyone who wants to think about the world differently from how we have been taught.[21]

But let's take another look at the religious conflicts plaguing contemporary societies and at the resources we could mine from ancient religions in these specific terms. In my opinion, if we truly seek the cash-value that polytheism can offer us today, we can find it especially in how it constructs a relationship with *the gods of others*. From this point of view ancient polytheism found its inspiration in *ways of thinking*[22] decidedly different from those pertaining to monotheism. Throughout this study, then, I will move forward by *comparing* the polytheistic ways of thinking with those of monotheism along the lines of the different reactions (and different results) produced every time they react to the conundrum represented by other people's gods. Why have I decided to use the comparative method? Because I am convinced that the exercise of comparison is the greatest tool for understanding cultural phenomena. As Alexis de Tocqueville wrote:

> One of the strangest failings of the human mind is its incapacity to understand objects, even observed in full sunlight, when they are not placed next to another object.[23]

This is why I will not hesitate to place cultural objects "side by side" throughout my study. Considering the spirit underlying this work, it is unnecessary to add that I will shy away from using abstract themes interesting only from the perspective of theoretical or intellectual debate; rather, I will choose topics relevant to the world we live in. In this spirit I will refrain from making preliminary statements of principle about monotheism and polytheism (I'll leave such an arduous task to others) as we start out on our journey, just as I will not interrogate today's neo-pagan and neo-polytheist movements, so popular in society and on the web.[24] I prefer to begin this story with two events from contemporary Italy, two moments that more than any others display the interaction between the cultural constructions that we intend to compare, side by side.

So now, *diis iuvantibus,* as the Romans would say: "may the gods help us."

CHAPTER ONE

Sacrificing the Nativity Scene and Bombing the Mosque

Just like in North America, it is quite common to set up nativity scenes at Christmastime in many European countries. In front of a papier-mâché landscape, small statues of sheep, shepherds, and many others are placed in a grotto that hosts Joseph, Mary, an ox, a donkey, and baby Jesus resting in a manger, all watched over by angels above. In Italy, this nativity scene is called a *presepio*, and it is very important on a socio-cultural level. Yet this cultural practice—itself so seemingly innocent—has become a point of bitter contention in Italy, where some schoolteachers and principals have decided to renounce the construction of nativity scenes so as not to upset the sensibilities of children and parents who do not participate in the Catholic tradition, Muslims in particular.

The choice to sacrifice this symbol of Christian festivities to the demands of religious multiculturalism provoked criticism from primarily right-leaning newspapers and opinion groups (the bottomless repository of the web still rings with their echoes), who lodged the accusation of wanting to sell out ancient traditions because they were too ready to accept an Islamized Italy.[1] On quite a different note, many thinkers within the Islamic community have made the effort to point out that for the Muslim faithful, a nativity scene represents nothing scandalous, given the consideration with which the Koran speaks about both Jesus and Mary.[2] I would like to state right up front that neither the contentious nor the conciliatory aspects of this debate interest me here.[3] My aim is, rather, an investigation into the *cultural motivations,* as I would like to call them, that may have led to the sacrifice of the nativity scene. These motivations extend beyond the borders of Italy and highlight a more general problem involving the relationship between different religions in the Western world.

At first glance, one might think that there is a French-style attitude behind this decision, in which the principle of secularism demands the removal of all religious symbols from public spaces.[4] In reality though, at least as these events were reported, less was said about the unsuitability of the object per se—as in: "nativity scenes, as an expression of religion, should not be found in public spaces"—than about the unease that this symbol might cause in children or adults who practice a religion other than Christianity. One might thus conclude that in a school where there were no children who practiced Islam or other religions, as was the norm in Italy before it became a nation of immigrants, nativity scenes could continue to be used without any objection. This decision therefore not only does not seem to be inspired by secular sentiments, but on the contrary, ascribes particular importance to religion and religious symbols, so much so as to eliminate symbols coming from one's own traditions so as not to hurt the feelings of people who do not share them. This kind of choice, it goes without saying, implies an attitude of great openness toward the cultures and religions of others. In other words, people who react this way not only accept—out of the principle of religious freedom—the practice of religions different from the traditional one of their country, but they actually choose—out of respect for other faiths—to avoid the display or imposition of their own or of the traditional religion. At this point have we reached the core of the cultural motivations upon which the sacrifice of the nativity scene is based? No, there is still more to unearth. In order to deepen my analysis, I would like to look at a contemporary event, reflecting, at least at first glance, a radically different attitude toward other people's faiths: the reactions sparked by the building of a mosque in Colle Val d'Elsa, a small historical hilltop town in Tuscany.

When permission was granted to erect the building, the world-renowned writer and journalist Oriana Fallaci went so far as to claim that she was ready to obtain explosives from her anarchist friends in Carrara: "I do not want to see a twenty-four-metre minaret in the landscape of Giotto. When I cannot even wear a cross or carry a Bible in their country! So I BLOW IT UP!," she stated in the *New Yorker*.[5] Far from renouncing the display of her own religious symbols, Fallaci proposed the elimination of those belonging to others: in a land where church bell towers are not scarce, the silhouette of a minaret seemed unacceptable to her. We have clearly passed from one extreme to the other, from the heights of religious tolerance to the heights of religious intolerance (it is unnecessary to indicate which of these two attitudes I would adopt if asked to choose one). Upon completion of the mosque, the polemics reignited, while arguments and rationales in defense of the choice, based upon the principle of religious freedom, arrived from the other side.[6]

But as with the sacrifice of the nativity scene, these are not the aspects of the affair that interest us; nor do we believe that it is sufficient to simply brand this sort of reaction as religious intolerance in order to explain and understand it, just as we found it insufficient to validate the previous example as religious tolerance. The important thing is not to pass judgment—in itself rather predictable—on these actions, but to identify their cultural motivations. And herein lies the crux of the matter. As different as these two choices seem, both of them—eliminating nativity scenes out of respect for Muslim children, removing a minaret from the Tuscan hills in tribute to our bell towers—paradoxically derive from the same *way of thinking:* the deeply-felt conviction, often so completely interiorized as to be unconscious, that there can be only one *single* and *unique* God.

This is an intrinsic principle of the three great monotheistic religions, and it derives from the *exclusive* nature originally characterizing the god of Israel: a unique God who neither accepts nor tolerates the existence of other gods before Him or apart from Him. Later we will return to the theme of this original "Mosaic distinction," as Jan Assmann defines it in his studies, and to its consequences.[7] Among the many Biblical affirmations of this principle, the words spoken by God to Moses while delivering the Laws, as written in the Book of Exodus, will suffice for the moment:

> I am the Lord your God, who brought you out of the land of Egypt, out of the house of slavery; *you shall have no other gods before me.* You shall not make for yourself an idol, whether in the form of anything that is in heaven above, or that is on the earth beneath, or that is in the water under the earth. You shall not bow down to them or worship them; for I the Lord your God *am a jealous God.*[8]

And here is what can be read further on in Exodus:

> Observe what I command you today [...]. Take care not to make a covenant with the inhabitants of the land to which you are going, or

> it will become a snare among you. *You shall tear down their altars, break their pillars, and cut down their sacred poles* (for you shall worship no other god, because *the Lord, whose name is Jealous, is a jealous God*).[9]

The "jealous god" will not allow for the existence of other gods; rather, he expressly invites his followers to destroy the religious symbols of others.

So here is the origin of the way of thinking under analysis: the conviction that there can be but one *single* and *unique* God, excluding all other divinities. "Thou shalt have no other gods before me" is, after all, the text of the first commandment as it is usually repeated within Christianity. The monotheistic religions have conflated the idea of "divinity" with that of "uniqueness" to such an extent that for the canonical heirs of these cultures, thinking of God inevitably means thinking of him as an entity that excludes the existence of another divinity or divinities. If it is God, this means he is "the only" God. Whoever has embraced this conviction, either out of true faith or out of a simple cultural habit descending from two thousand years of Western monotheism, possesses a potential range of reactions when confronted by another religion, reactions that fall between the two extremes we identified above: renouncing one's own religious symbols so as not to offend those who profess a different faith (the principle of maximum religious tolerance), taking for granted that for the "others" also there can be only one God, *theirs*; or eliminating the religious symbols of others, precisely as the God of Israel said to do (principle of maximum religious intolerance), since there can be only one God, *ours*. What is difficult, if not impossible, to conceive, due to the ways of thinking produced by an exclusivist monotheism, is the possibility of worshiping *two* or *more* divinities at the same time: in a word, that we can be *polytheists*.

And yet, polytheism (I will look more closely at what this term means later on) was for centuries the religious form practiced by the ancient peoples: Babylonians, Assyrians, Egyptians, Greeks, Etruscans, Romans, and so forth; just as millions of people living on our planet today practice polytheistic religions. Nevertheless the ways of venerating the divine by this vast population are largely ignored except by religious historians or anthropologists, while popular culture never speaks of them, nor does it think it useful or necessary to know anything about them. Even less do we bother to learn anything about the opinion that these populations may have about monotheism, and yet it would be both interesting and proper to know it.[10] Returning to the two concrete examples I started with, being polytheistic would mean that the same person, at the same time, could celebrate both Christmas, with its nativity scene, and Ramadan: one could choose to venerate the divine both in the Church of St. Catherine in Colle Val d'Elsa and in the mosque just built in that same town. Or even walk out of one and go straight into the other.

According to this logic, then, the teachers who sacrificed the nativity scene to religious multiculturalism believed that Muslim children, faithful to their one single and unique god, could only respond with embarrassment to another god, equally single and unique to another religion. One they certainly could not consider a god since God can only be only one, their own. For this reason they decided not to put up nativity scenes. They showed great cultural awareness in doing so, yes, but their actions are not any less determined by monotheistic ways of thinking. The same ways of thinking, in practice, although inverted 180 degrees, motivated the religious intolerance (equally monotheistic) of Oriana Fallaci and her followers. The root of the problem lies in our cultural inability to be polytheists, to imagine *together* and *contemporaneously* multiple different divinities that integrate within the same religious system and even identify with other foreign divinities.

CHAPTER TWO

Festivity Figurines

Animals, Shepherds, Three Kings

We are now standing in front of a nativity scene. What do we see? As previously noted, a *presepio* is a large or small collection of figurines placed around a miniature landscape, the size and complexity of which can vary significantly.

The ideal center of this inhabited landscape is a grotto (or hut) inside of which we find the representation of baby Jesus lying in a manger (or crib) watched over by Mary and Joseph; slightly behind them, in the background, we find an ox and a donkey. Above the grotto the angels announce the birth of Jesus on small strips of paper. On top of it all there is the conventional reproduction of a star or comet. All around, distanced to varying degrees from the center of the action, are small statuettes representing sheep, shepherds, and a wide range of different trades or social roles: farmers, millers, washerwomen, blacksmiths, water-carriers, innkeepers, travelers, and so on, depending on the imagination of whomever built the nativity scene, on local traditions, or simply on the availability of figurines.

On the Twelfth Night, January 6, the day of Epiphany, three statues of people dressed in a decidedly Eastern manner finally make their appearance at the grotto or hut: the three kings, or Magi, accompanied by an equally exotic entourage. Depending on the various local or even family traditions—or if the nativity scene is large enough to allow it—the Magi are made to effectively "travel" day after day with their caravan moving progressively closer until they are placed directly in front of the grotto. In general, at least one of the Magi kneels next to baby Jesus.

As is very clear, the nativity scene occupies a starring role within Christian culture, insofar as every year it reenacts one of its foundational events: the birth of the Savior. Using a complicated combination of miniature artifacts—representing people and animals, papier-mâché cliffs, grottoes, and bluffs, tinfoil rivers, fields of dried moss, all interacting with the birth image—the nativity scene re-articulates the entire narrative. But is this traditional product of household ingenuity nothing more than a fairy-tale retelling of the Gospel story? Embellished by details as poetic as they are ingenious? On the contrary, the nativity scene constitutes the authentic "cultural memory"[1] of the Savior's birth, the ways in which tradition has built upon the scarce details of the canonical Gospel narratives: texts actually known by very few, while everyone, or nearly everyone, remembers and knows what a nativity scene *says.* The message is delivered more efficiently because the artifacts representing the ingredients of this metaphorical narrative—the hut, the statuettes, the papier-mâché background—have been directly *manipulated* to this aim. The nativity scene is not merely a reproduction of cultural memory, but an *interaction* with it. The reactions sparked by the decision to sacrifice this complex and traditional practice show that it is so much more than an insignificant act.

The historical, cultural, and textual events that brought about the creation of the nativity scene—itself articulated in various different local, national, or denominational forms—are too intricate to attempt even a brief summary. Nor would this fit within the purpose of the work at hand.[2] If, as I maintain, cultural memory is embodied in the *presepio*, what truly interests me is to shine some light on some of the meanings that a nativity scene is able to communicate synchronically: through the simple, visible presence of certain elements and the system of relationships generated between them.

Let me begin with the ox and the donkey situated next to the son of God in order to warm him and protect him. They do not exist as a narrative element in the canonical Gospel stories, yet they are generally recognized as some of the most characteristic parts of the nativity scene. When St. Francis, in the village of Greccio, founded this tradition, he had "a manger (*praesepium*) prepared, hay brought in, and an ox and donkey led to it."[3] These two animals, located directly next to the Savior, are the signifiers of a cultural message that is anything but irrelevant. As a matter of fact, their presence places baby Jesus in a vast multitude of mythical children who, after having been expelled and persecuted by the human community that gave them life, are accepted and protected by animals, allowing them to one day become the founders of a new civilization. Just think of Cyrus the Great, a child abandoned in the wild and protected by a dog; or of Romulus and Remus, nursed by a she-wolf; or of a young Zeus who, threatened by Cronos, was fed by a nanny goat in a grotto in Crete. And I could mention many other heroes of antiquity and the medieval period. In this framework, the "natural world" itself, represented by the helpful animals, attests to the exceptional quality of the tiny hero by virtue of his spontaneous and incontestable authority.[4] Even baby Jesus—forced to be born in a manger because he was excluded from human homes (*locus non erat eis in deversorio*) and then immediately threatened with death by Herod[5]—is protected and kept warm by two animals whose "natural" devotion to the child offers an implicit demonstration of his divine nature, as officially announced by the angels. Consider how the Gospel of Luke is very scanty with detail: there is no specific mention of the location in which Jesus' birth takes place. It recounts only that the infant was placed in a manger, leaving us to suppose that Mary and Joseph were thus inside a stable. And yet the narration of the nativity scene often places the child inside a grotto, as inhospitable a place as any, primitive, representing remoteness from human culture and surrounded by nature.[6] Nature is another element, represented in part by the animal protectors, connecting baby Jesus to the mythical children who must overcome the harshness of uncivilized nature at the beginning of their path toward the foundation of a new civilization.

What about the variety of crafts and trades displayed around the grotto? The characters are engaged in widely diverse activities. Such a range of social roles serves to signify the universality of the Christian annunciation, expressed by a miniature sampling of the vast humanity for whom it is intended. *They're all here,* it seems to say, witnesses and beneficiaries of the event. It is also worth pointing out that compared to the weavers, blacksmiths, or laundresses, shepherds play a privileged role. The latter are traditionally located "closer" than the others to the legendary grotto. The topographical distribution of the figures, not only their social meaning, is a tool aimed at conveying cultural memory. The presence of shepherds at the moment of birth is explicitly written in the Gospel of Luke.[7] But it is difficult not to think that their importance in the nativity scene is connected with their closer proximity to the simple life, to nature, and to the animal world. As such, they and their sheep are better suited to witness the goodness and the truth of the annunciation. This is why their proper place is "closer" to the grotto or hut. Once we open the question of the truths communicated by the nativity scene, though, there is, in particular, one more that I need to examine, because it brings us directly back to the topic I started from: the sacrifice of this tradition out of respect for practitioners of another faith.

As mentioned, on January 6, the day of Epiphany, the statuettes of the Magi are placed next to the child: three distinguished personages come from afar to kneel in front of Jesus. In the text of the Gospel of Matthew, the only one of the canonical gospels to mention them, they are called *mágoi,* a word in Greek with two meanings: first, specifically the high priests or sages of Persia; second, and more generically, "magicians" or "wizards," even in the pejorative sense of "charlatans." The text of Matthew gives an additional clarification of the term *mágoi: ex anatolón,* "from the East."[8] So who are these three men from the East (in the nativity scene they are identified as such by their clothing) kneeling in front of the child? The question has less to do with the "real" meaning of these figures in the Gospel of Matthew[9] than it does with how they have been transformed into nativity scene figurines by cultural memory. Through this evolution, the original *mágoi*—the priests of ancient Persia, the wise men who hold the secrets of magic and astrology—have become "kings," all the while remaining "Magi": a designation that evokes connections with other or distant religions and arcane knowledge. Guided by the divine sign of a star (the painted silver star hanging over the papier-mâché grotto), come to venerate the child and give precious gifts to him, these exotic characters express the honor bestowed by Eastern religions upon baby Jesus.

Let us not be tricked, though, by our cultural knowledge related to the nativity scene narrative. Placing these three new characters next to the manger on Twelfth Night is not meant merely to give further proof of the divine nature of the child, like the ones already displayed by other actors within the scene. Proclaimed as God by the angels, recognized as such by the animals, shepherds, and so forth, and at the same time honored and adored by the Magi—representatives of the Eastern religions—Jesus appears not only as *a* god but as *the* god: the only true one, in front of whom other religions must step aside now that he has come to manifest himself amongst mankind. Melchior, Caspar, and Balthazar, placed in the nativity scene at the apex of its narrative cycle, bring something else to the demonstration of the divine nature of Jesus: a denial of non-Christian religions and the avowal of his exclusive truth. A denial and an avowal expressed in a good-natured, almost fairy-tale manner,[10] but no less definitive because of this. The memory of the ancient Mosaic distinction, the persuasion that there is room for just one single and true God, is not to be found only in the feelings or in the unconscious convictions of whomever is building a *presepio*: it is an integral part of it.

CHAPTER THREE

End of the Year Figurines

Sigilla, Sigillaria, and *Compitalia*

It is no simple task to find ancient parallels for the nativity scene, considering the large chronological and cultural gap that separates the ancient and the medieval and modern worlds, but it is nonetheless an experiment worth trying. Identifying polytheistic practices in some way resembling the nativity scene could allow a comparison with this Christian symbol, following the same methodology I presented at the beginning of my study. I must try to find some relevant Roman "cultural object" to place next to the nativity scene. To identify it, I must start from the most characteristic traits of this Christian symbol: the *time of year* in which it is done, at the end of December; the decisive presence of religious *figurines;* and the *familial* or domestic context of this practice. The nativity scene is at the center of the holiday system of the Twelve Days of Christmas. Within the relations celebrated during the holidays a decisive role is played generally by the people who are dear to us—who come together in order to exchange greetings and gifts—and especially by *children,*[1] who not only are the primary recipients of the gifts so important to this ritual, but who also enjoy direct representation *within* the nativity scene through the child god at the very center of it.

In Rome, at the end of December, all the population, free and slave, celebrated a holiday in honor of the god Saturn, the *Saturnalia* festival. During this festival they also celebrated the *Sigillaria,* seven days when small pottery or wax figurines called *sigilla,* "small icons" dedicated to Saturn, were put on sale in the annual market held at this time. Alongside the *sigilla,* one could buy other objects, such as toys, books, candles, or platters and other small gifts meant to be given to friends, just like the *sigilla.* We even know that on the occasion of the *Sigillaria,* children were given money specifically in order to make their own purchases at the market.[2] The exchange of gifts amongst loved ones and the attention paid especially to children—two acts that evoke the atmosphere of the family hearth—both constitute points of contact between *Sigillaria* and the activities associated with Christmas in the subsequent culture. What strikes me even more, though, is the similar use in both holidays of pottery figurines. It becomes rather difficult not to see a functional parallel between the ancient *Sigillaria* market, where the votive figurines were sold, and modern Christmas stalls with their wares of figurines destined for nativity scenes. The workshops of San Gregorio Armeno in Naples, with their wondrous selection of shepherds and other statuettes, seem to find a quite unexpected antecedent in ancient Rome.

Let's move on. At the end of *Saturnalia* and the concomitant *Sigillaria,* around New Year's Eve (December 31), the Romans celebrated another holiday of interest to us. The *Compitalia* was held once a year on a date solemnly declared every year by the praetor one week prior to the event. This festival was in honor of the Lares, the house-gods that more and better than any others embodied the domestic life of the Romans, and as such were honored indiscriminately by all members of the *familia,* be they free or slave. At *Compitalia,* though, the festival was not celebrated by separate family groups, but by the wider community formed by everyone who lived near the same *compitum,* the same crossroads: what we might call members of the same "neighborhood." People, then, who were united by particularly close relationships even if they didn't belong to the same family.[3] In honor of the *Lares compitales,* the neighborhood would decorate the images of these divinities with balls of yarns (*pilae*) and small dolls (*maniae*) inside the shrines built in their honor, and we know that slaves, as they were during the *Saturnalia,* were allowed certain liberties during the celebrations.[4] Just a few days after *Sigillaria,* still another holiday followed in Rome, focusing on ties between people with close relationships in which we find other statuettes: not only the statuettes of the Lares but also the *maniae* used to decorate the shrines. One could thus say that during the period between the old and the new year, ancient Rome (like Christian Europe with its nativity scene) experienced a blooming of statuettes and figurines around which a system of relationships of a religious, familial, and emotional nature were established, similar to the Twelve Days of Christmas.

But Rome was similar to one of our contemporary metropolises, home to men and women of various ethnic and cultural origins, and whose religious beliefs inclined toward a plurality of gods. This is why the comparison is even more significant. Do you think someone might suggest not opening the *Sigillaria* market because the *sigilla,* linked to the cult of Saturn, would offend (for lack of a better word) the followers of Cybele? Or could you imagine that some of the "neighbors" might decide not to decorate the *Lares of Compitalia* with *maniae* and *pilae,* or even to remove their images from the shrines so as to not offend the sentiments of any eventual devotees of Isis who lived near the same *compitum?* Certainly not, simply because in the Roman world, gods could be integrated rather than excluded. During *Saturnalia,* Saturn was worshipped, for the festival of *Compitalia* the *Lares compitales* were worshipped, and after these—or before them, or during them—there were other celebrations for other gods deemed worthy of worship.

CHAPTER FOUR

A Life Through Figurines

The *Lararium*

It is not quite yet time to abandon the world of figurines. A closer look at the *Lararium* of a Roman house, the space where the statues of the Lares were kept, can still bring further elements for the comparison I am conducting between ancient and modern religious figurines.

The *Lararium* was, in essence, a shrine that could be placed in different parts of the *domus* depending on the time of year or local traditions: in the atrium, the kitchen, the bedroom, and so forth.[1] What did it contain? The figures of the Lares, first and foremost, but as we will see, other representations too. Most importantly, this collection of statuettes, grouped in an intimate domestic niche, expressed a particular religious and cultural message. At times it told a genuine "story" similar to the nativity scene, although its character was personal rather than a collective one about the salvation of humanity. However, there is another important comparative divide that runs between the nativity scene and the *Lararium*.

Let me begin with the statuettes of the household gods: the Lares. There are numerous extant examples. Ordinarily, a Lar is represented as a young man dressed in a short tunic above the knees, clearly cinched at the waist. In one hand he holds a *rhytón*, a chalice shaped like a horn, and in the other a *patera*, a small offering dish. In Pompeii, the Lares are shown in pairs, with symmetrical poses, with the figure of *Genius* in the middle. The position in which they are shown suggests a slight dancing movement, and overall their poses convey a feeling of joy and happiness.[2] As stated before, though, a *Lararium* was not meant only for the figures of the Lares. Cicero recounts that in Heius's *Lararium* in Messina, there were four statues, each quite valuable: a Cupid made by Praxiteles, a Hercules made by Myron, and two figures of *canephorae*, the "basket carriers" in Greek processions. Cupid and Hercules were evidently gods to whom Heius, for reasons both religious and aesthetic (so it would seem), was particularly devoted, and as such, were different from those that might be found in the *Lararium* of other people. In the one owned by Trimalchio for example (as told by Petronius), there were "silver Lares, a marble Venus, and a golden casket by no means small, which held, so they told us, the first shavings of Trimalchio's beard."[3]

Different gods then shared a single dwelling space. Jumping ahead a few decades, in the Emperor Hadrian's *Lararium* there was a rare statuette—a gift from Suetonius[4]—representing his imperial predecessor Augustus when he still used the *cognomen* of Thurinus. Moving ahead again, the Emperor Marcus Aurelius's *Lararium* tells still another story. As is well known, he was a philosopher, and as such the disciple of many teachers from his era: Sextus of Chaeronea, the nephew or grandson of Plutarch, Arulenus Rusticus, Claudius Maximus, and Cinna Catulus,

Stoics, and the Peripatetic Gnaeus Claudius Severus Arabianus. But he was most devoted to Iunius Rusticus, whom he twice named Consul and for whom he asked the Senate to erect statues after his death. The biographer of Marcus concludes:

> On his teachers in general, moreover, he conferred great honors, for he even kept golden statues of them in his [*Lararium*].[5]

It is clear that the figures kept in a *Lararium* reflected not only their owners' religious orientation through the images of specific gods, but could even display their philosophical choices and their education. This shrine was a *place* where veneration of the gods intersected with autobiography, both personal (Trimalchio's beard) and cultural (Marcus Aurelius's teachers). Something comparable to a private diary, in iconographic form, of individual inclinations, emotions, and experiences.

As time passes one can encounter yet another emperor's *Lararium,* that of Severus Alexander. As his biographer recounts:

> if it were permissible, that is to say, if he had not lain with his wife, in the early morning hours he would worship in the sanctuary of his Lares, in which he kept statues of the deified emperors—of whom, however, only the best had been selected—and also of certain holy souls, among them Apollonius, and, according to a contemporary writer, Christ, Abraham, Orpheus, and others of this same character and, besides, the portraits of his ancestors.[6]

Alexander's *Lararium,* in turn, had its own particular composition. The figures it included told of the public milieu (past emperors) and private life (the ancestors) of its owner, as well as his—might we say—spirituality, placing Apollonius alongside Christ, Abraham, and Orpheus. A few pages later in the text, Severus's biographer tells us how the emperor even kept an image of Alexander the Great, "enshrined in his greater *Lararium* along with the most righteous men and the deified emperors," and a "second *Lararium*" hosted the images of Virgil and Cicero, and "had portraits of Achilles and the great heroes."[7] The Lararium—in this case we had better say the Lararia since there were two of them—was a place dedicated to *pluralism* in every sense of the word. It was perfectly natural that amongst these statuettes, ranging from poets to the heroes of epic poetry, from great military leaders of the past to the gods, one might even include figures from two different religious systems: Christ and Orpheus. It could not have been otherwise.

It is also worth noting that none of these figures were included to pay homage or to bow down to the "*one*" that represented the "true" and "only" god, as happens with the kneeling Magi in front of baby Jesus. This difference between the Christian nativity scene and the Roman *Lararium*, when placed side by side, brings to light once again the corresponding difference between monotheistic and polytheistic ways of thinking: imagining one God exclusively, rather than imagining *the gods* with no hierarchy within a religious landscape able to bring together statues of ancestors, god-like emperors, philosophers, poets and writers, heroes, saints, and moral guides.

CHAPTER FIVE

Thou Shalt Have No Other God Before Me

Jan Assmann's interpretation of the forms of Judaic monotheism and its founding principles is one of the most interesting theories presented in recent years in the field of historical and anthropological research on religion.[1] The scholar combined different historical realities and models, especially the Egyptian, the Judaic and the Mesopotamian, with Freudian analysis and the European history of religious and theological studies starting from the seventeenth century onward. It is not a simple task to encapsulate Assmann's thought in a few words but in extremely concise terms, this is what he says.

Judaic monotheism is a "counter-religion," it establishes itself as truth, denouncing all others as false and as such delegitimizing all pagan gods.

The distinction between true and false in religion finds its expression in the story of Exodus, in the form of the separation of the Israelites from the Egyptians, under the leadership of Moses. Moses himself establishes an alliance with God: the Israelites will acknowledge God as their redeemer and obey His law, refusing to worship the images of other divinities, as shown in the passages previously cited.[2] The prohibition against worshiping other gods presupposes that, in the beginning, nobody contested the reality of foreign gods. This is the only way to explain Yahweh's "jealousy" toward them. This is the period defined by Othmar Keel as "immature monotheism."[3] During the subsequent eras of cultural history, this relationship with the gods of others would evolve, arriving at the point of considering them completely false gods, or demons, when compared with the true God, the only one who deserves such a name.

The next part of Assmann's theory makes reference to an earlier experiment in monotheism carried out by the pharaoh Amenhotep IV (who called himself Akhenaten) and the famous essay by Sigmund Freud on Moses and monotheism.[4] But in my opinion, the most enduring element of Assmann's work is having clearly presented evidence that Judaic monotheism implicates an *exclusivist* nature. The God of the Israelites is a unique, jealous god who cannot bear the presence of other gods "before him," and as such asks his worshippers to make a choice: one cannot venerate *many* gods, as was the norm in Egypt or in ancient Mesopotamia, but only one. In this framework, the relationship between different religions is forced into a position of "true" and "false": the religion practiced by the Israelites is true, while the others are simply false religions. Practicing them is thus equivalent to a mistake, one that will be severely punished by a jealous God. This original "Mosaic distinction," as Assmann has repeatedly called it, is the basis for the other, equally exclusive, distinctions introduced by later versions of monotheism, such as that between "Christian" and "pagan," or "Muslim" and "infidel."[5] The "Mosaic distinction" thus played a fundamental role in the creation of religions that developed out of Judaism. Considering the importance of

Christianity and Islam in the contemporary world, this "exclusive zeal for the truth of religion"[6] (as Edward Gibbon defined it) carries a significance that goes well beyond mere theoretical reflections about religious phenomena. It touches the feelings, the behavior, and the lives of millions of people.

Conceiving the god-relationship as exclusive and radically oppositional has, over the course of history, notoriously resulted in tragic consequences. This choice has led populations into acts of religious violence, into a hostility toward all those who refuse to worship the "true" and "only" God.[7] As we all know, the monotheistic religions based on the "Mosaic distinction" have disgracefully adopted this characteristic with particular enthusiasm, repeatedly waging wars, persecutions, and violence in the name of God, and continuing to do so in certain parts of the world (as we learn almost every day in the news).

I will try to compare monotheism and polytheism within the more limited context of religious violence. A substantial difference comes immediately into view: while the Greeks and Romans were as violent and bloodthirsty as the cultures of later centuries, they never acted this way out of religious motivations or in order to avow the truth of a single god. This is such a striking, such an obvious fact that it usually ends up going unnoticed, like the famous *Purloined letter* in the story by Edgar Allan Poe, hiding in plain sight. Maybe our reluctance to acknowledge this truth is caused by the fact that it would be almost embarrassing to point it out.[8] And yet what other reaction would one expect when faced with the evidence that the ancients never started a war in order to validate one religion over another, in contrast to what Christians and Muslims did throughout the following centuries? As Marc Augé wrote:

> Although polytheistic societies were harsh societies, societies that raised the question of violence amongst themselves—and even though religion was connected to all of the power relationships that create a social network—religion could nonetheless never be considered the "cause" for violence.[9]

I will examine in greater depth the specific cultural motivations at the basis of this remarkable absence (as it seems to contemporary monotheistic or post-monotheistic eyes), but it is easy to see how the root of this behavior lies primarily in the *plural* qualities of the gods. If I start from a situation where there are many gods, and "my own" gods are equally multiple, then the inclination to claim that the gods of others are non-divinities, false gods, or demons becomes less likely. As David Hume had already pointed out in the middle of the eighteenth century, it was precisely the pluralism of the divine and the absence of a single, unique god that had made the various gods, ceremonies, traditions, and rituals of diverse peoples of antiquity seem "compatible."[10]

If we consider the Mosaic distinction once again, we can see how this produced centuries of conflicts, persecutions, and religious violence under Christian hegemony. But the uniqueness and exclusiveness of the Christian God seems to have lost a good part of its intransigence over time when compared to its older version. Evidence of this can be found in the current *Catechism of the Catholic Church,* a document that, one can reasonably surmise, reflects Church doctrine in its most widely accepted and shared form, far from extreme views and overly sophisticated theological arguments.[11] In fact, there is no mention of either the "jealous God" or of the requirement to tear down the idols and altars of other religions in this document. Yet the exclusiveness and uniqueness of the Christian God remains constant. The interpretation of the first commandment begins with the passage from Exodus just quoted—"I am the Lord your God, who brought you out of the land of Egypt, out of the house of slavery; you shall have no other gods before me. You shall not make for yourself an idol, whether in the form of anything that is in heaven above, or that is on the earth beneath, or that is in the water under the earth. You shall not bow down to them or worship them"—albeit with the removal of the reference to a "jealous God"—and continues on by reaffirming that "*the one and true God* first reveals his glory to Israel."[12] Following this statement there is, however, a section entitled "The social responsibility of religion and the right to religious freedom," which gives evidence of a new and different openness toward other religions. The articles of interest here are basically constituted by a synthesis of various Second Vatican Council resolutions, placed in quotation marks:

> 'All men are bound to seek the *truth,* especially in what concerns God and his Church, and to embrace it and hold on to it as they come to know it.' This duty derives from 'the very dignity of the human person.' It does not contradict a 'sincere respect' for different religions which frequently '*reflect a ray* of that *truth* which enlightens all men,' nor the requirement of charity, which urges Christians 'to treat with love, prudence and patience those who are in *error* or *ignorance* with regard to the faith.'[13]

The contents of this article certainly appear to be directed toward moderation and openness, but the "truth"—which all men are bound to seek by natural instinct, it would seem—is still the God of the Catholic Church. We are forced to conclude that everything that falls outside this boundary is in the realm of falsehood. Compared with the ancient Biblical versions, the disdain toward other religions has certainly been exchanged for respect, and hostility replaced by charity. But this does not change that whoever practices a religion different from Christianity is nonetheless in "error" and "ignorance." Non-Christians will be respected depending on their possibility to grasp a "ray" of "truth," able to lead them to a future affinity with Catholic religion. Making reference to other Councils and encyclicals, in later sections the *Catechism* returns to the theme of the "truth," "uniqueness," and "authenticity" of the Christian religion, from which derives the obligation of Christians to practice evangelism, to seek the active conversion of others to the one true religion:

> The duty of offering God *genuine worship* concerns man both individually and socially. This is 'the traditional Catholic teaching on the moral duty of individuals and societies toward the *true religion* and the one Church of Christ.' *By constantly evangelizing men,* the Church works toward enabling them 'to infuse the Christian spirit into the mentality and mores, laws and structures of the communities in which [they] live.' The social duty of Christians is to respect and awaken in each man the love of the true and the good. It requires them to make known the worship of the *one true religion* which subsists in the Catholic and apostolic Church. Christians are called to be the light of the world. Thus, the Church shows forth the *kingship of Christ* over all creation and in particular over human societies. 'Nobody may be forced to act against his convictions, nor is anyone to be restrained from acting in accordance with his conscience in religious matters in private or in public, alone or in association with others, within due limits.' This right is based on the very nature of the human person, whose dignity enables him freely to assent to the divine truth which transcends the temporal order. For this reason it 'continues to exist even in those who *do not live up to their obligation of seeking the truth* and adhering to it.'[14]

I will try to outline the method by which, in this page of the *Catechism,* the relationship with someone who practices a different religion is laid out. On one side there is the confirmation of the "truth," "uniqueness," and "authenticity" of Catholic religion, with the resulting "kingship" of Christ over all creation; on the other, a declaration that in religious matters, no one can be forced to act against his or her convictions, all the while reconfirming that those who do not follow Catholicism are not only in error, but they are not even trying to correct themselves, as the "obligation of seeking the truth" would have them do.

CHAPTER SIX

Translating the Gods, Translating God

I have chosen these passages from the *Catechism* not merely to underline how the ancient Mosaic distinction lives on in the current Catholic interpretation of the first commandment, or to point out how far contemporary Christianity has distanced itself from the original harshness.[1] They serve, rather, to compare the image of God presented in these texts and some of the standard practices used by polytheistic systems to interact with the gods and religions of other people.

I must therefore return to Jan Assmann's work. In his research, Assmann did not restrict himself to demonstrating the exclusivist nature of Yahweh or of the later monotheistic religions, but formulated yet another important observation. As a unique and exclusive divinity, the God of monotheistic religions is not "translatable" into any other god. In other words, within these religious systems it is logically impossible to say that God (the entity that *we* indicate by this name) corresponds to or is recognizable as any other god venerated by other cultures. The ancient polytheistic religions, on the other hand, worked in the opposite manner, specifically allowing adherents to identify common traits among gods belonging to different peoples, even going so far as to eventually recognize them as one and the same. The ancient civilizations of the near East have literally left us "translation" charts in this regard. For example, the *Anu ša Ameli* list is formulated in three columns, the first of which gives Sumerian names, the second Akkadian names, and the third the role or sphere of influence of each god; in other words, the *tertium comparationis* that makes it possible to understand the link between separate gods. There is also an "explanatory list" that includes the names of gods in the languages of the Amorites, Hurrians, Elamites, and Kassites, as well as in Sumerian and Akkadian, through which it is possible to make connections even between gods belonging to decidedly different religious cultures.[2]

This should come as no surprise, since we know that the Romans associated a number of their gods with Greek gods. Latin writers and poets commonly called *Ártemis* by the name of *Diana, Poséidon* as *Neptunus, Zéus* as *Iuppiter,* and so on. They even gave the Roman gods attributes belonging to the Hellenic ones, and turned them into the characters of mythological stories that had originally been told about the gods of Greece, as was the case with Ovid's *Metamorphoses.* Western culture—as an offshoot of Roman culture and heir to the image of the Greeks created by the Romans [3]—continued in this same vein for centuries: if Botticelli painted the "Birth of Venus" (and not Aphrodite) and Bernini sculpted the "Rape of Proserpina" (and not Persephone or Kore), John Keats did not hesitate to dedicate a poem to "Apollo and the Graces" (and not the Charites), and Percy Bysshe Shelley, translating the Homeric Hymn to Aphrodite, called Minerva (not Athena) the daughter of Zeus. The Roman habit of assimilating and identifying their own gods with those of the Greeks has had wide-ranging and long-lasting consequences, so much so as to indelibly mark our own perception of the ancient religious universe, particularly the Greek one.

The figurative and literary tradition we have inherited has so thoroughly accustomed us to this game of similarity and substitution that we run the risk of finding it all quite normal. It becomes immediately less so, though, when we consider that for the Greeks and the Romans, names like Athena and Minerva, Hera and Juno and so forth, did not correspond to generic characters from "classical mythology" thrown around by poets, artists, or bored high school students, which is what they became after the arrival of Christianity.[4] *Athéna* and *Minerva, Hèra* and *Iuno* were real, powerful gods to whom entire cities dedicated majestic ceremonies in the various temples erected in their honor. In spite of this, the Greek gods could be "translated" into their corresponding Roman gods, all the while preserving their own specificity in regards to ceremonies and rituals, offerings and sacrifices.

A parallel practice toward the Roman gods was even adopted by the Greeks, particularly after Rome became the capital of an empire that included Greece and the Hellenized peoples. Authors like Dionysius of Halicarnassus or Plutarch, who wrote works intended to illustrate Roman culture and history in the Greek language, had no scruples in calling the Roman *Venus* by the name of *Aphrodíte* or in giving the appellation of *Héroes* to the *Lares.* In fact, Plutarch's *Life of Romulus* or Dionysius's *Roman Antiquity* demand constant attention from the reader, a continuous readiness to decode the Greek names given to Roman gods. Even this might lead us into a mental error: well, they were Greeks, of course they acted this way!

However, if instead of the *Life of Theseus* we were reading a translation of prophet Salih's biography in his efforts to turn the inhabitants of Thamud (today's Yemen) away from the practice of idol worship, we would never find an expression like this: "O my people! Worship God the Father, you have no other God but Him!" (instead of the original "O my people! Worship Allah, you have no other Ilah [god] but Him!").[5]

On the contrary, the readers of Plutarch or Dionysius not only must pay attention to the Greek names of Roman gods, but must be very careful and ready to decode the tendency of these authors to translate into Greek even the Latin nouns for Roman institutions such as the *senatus* (*gerousía*) or magistracies as the *praetura* (*strategía*). This tendency offers an additional glimpse into the dominant ways of thinking in ancient polytheism, where the gods were translated *in the same manner* as political and legal institutions. In a polytheistic world, the gods were hardly "unique," exceptional, and exclusive, and thus when it came to describing or explaining them to people who came from a different culture and spoke another language, they were translated just as a public office or institution.

This polytheistic possibility of translating one god into another, even across different populations and cultures, thus corresponds to a flexible attitude, spontaneously capable of creating integration and fusion, not separation, between different religious systems.

Even when we leave the ancient world behind we find evidence for this same phenomenon in other polytheisms. For example, local gods in Japan, belonging to more ancient religious traditions, became associated with Shinto or Buddhist divinities.[6] Using a metaphor from the field of economics, we could say that a kind of common market of the gods existed in the ancient world, an exchangeability of the divine, distinguished by the possibility of finding commonalities between various religious "currencies" belonging to different peoples. It would be best to specify immediately, though, that this game of associations between gods was not only practiced among cultures marked by a particular "closeness" or "cultural intimacy,"[7] like the Greeks and Romans, but also with regard to more distant cultures. I will quote some examples.

A traveler in the early centuries of our era who found his way into the sanctuary of Augusta Treverorum, the ancient name of Trier, would have made an interesting discovery. Among the many gods worshipped there, this traveler would have encountered one called *Vertumnus sive Pisintus,* "Vertumnus otherwise known as Pisintus." What an odd name: who was he? We know of Vertumnus. He is an Etruscan god who became Roman, was worshiped in the most ancient heart of Rome, and became legendary for his capacity for metamorphosis. What was such a Roman god doing in the Rhineland-Palatinate in that specific age? And who was this Pisintus who, it seems, accounted for the other half of his identity? A Gallic god, about whom we actually know nothing, but with whom the Roman Vertumnus was associated: the perfect way to exemplify the fusion between local peoples and Roman colonizers, almost as if beyond language and customs, the two populations had also chosen to meld their gods.[8] To Vertumnus's example, associated with the Gallic Pisintus, I could also add the German Wotan associated with Mercurius or Thincsus with Mars; the Egyptian Serapis associated with Jupiter and Asclepius, and so on; on the Greek side, Herodotus had already claimed that the Scythians called Hestia by the name of Tabitis, Zeus as Papais, and Apollo as Ghetosiros; while we know that on the Egyptian side Isis was often given the name of Athena.[9] The translation of the gods was thus like the spokes of a wheel, a sextant used full circle to help find one's way within the religious universe of others and to define the relationships that "our" religious system had with it. And this took place well beyond the degree to which economic, political, commercial, and artistic relationships were active between the populations in question.[10] As we will see later on, the translation of the gods and goddesses represented not only a final result of intercultural relations, but also a starting point for them.

I will try now to end my comparison. Given the extent to which polytheistic systems were pliable in carrying out the reciprocal translation of gods and goddesses belonging to different peoples and cultures, would it have been possible to act the same way with the god described in the passages of the *Catechism* quoted above?

As I have shown, Catholic Christianity is presented as the "true" religion and all men, guided by their very "nature," are not only driven to seek this "truth" but are also exhorted to embrace it and pass it along to others. In addition, there is the reiteration of the "authentic practice"—the Catholic one—that one is bound to undertake for God, and the explicit affirmation that the Church, through the work of Christian evangelists, manifests the "kingship" of Christ over all creation and all human societies. Ideas such as "truth," "authenticity," and "nature" are absolutes. How could *two* truths or *two* authenticities exist at the same time? *Two* natures could coexist even less. A "second truth" can be nothing but a falsehood, just as a "second authenticity" is certainly a counterfeit of the first; while a being who follows the impulses of "two natures" can only be a hybrid. The same argument stands for the political (shall we say) representation of the "truth" of Catholicism, that affirmation of the "kingship" of Christ over all creation and all humankind. Can a sovereign who enjoys absolute power, total dominion over all existence, be "translated" or associated with another sovereign? He would no longer be an absolute monarch. As we see, even in its gentler version, mitigated by centuries of debate over religious tolerance and the freedom of worship, the construction of the divine figure in Catholicism maintains the "Mosaic distinction" as its defining characteristic, and with it, its untranslatability.

CHAPTER SEVEN

Grammatical Paradoxes

The Name of God

Titus Flavius Josephus, the Jewish nobleman who became part of the imperial entourage after the end of the war against the Romans (first century CE), wrote the following in his *Contra Apionem:*

> Now I have no mind to make an inquiry into the laws of other nations. For the custom of our country is to keep our own laws, but not to bring accusations against the laws of others. And indeed our legislator hath expressly forbidden us to laugh at and revile those that are esteemed gods by other people; on account of the very name of God ascribed to them (*autès héneka prosegorías toú theoú*).[1]

Josephus not only shows his feelings of respect toward the gods venerated by other people in this passage, he also seems to attribute his attitude directly to the Legislator, who is none other than Moses: the very same Moses who, amongst the many laws he delivered to the Israelites, included one that mandated respectful behavior toward the gods of others. Josephus's claim is based on a verse included in Exodus, in the Septuagint translation, that does sound something like "you shall not speak disrespectfully about the gods."[2] Understandably, such a commandment can be perplexing. It appears in the same book in which the Lord not only declares his jealousy and imposes exclusive worship for his people ("thou shalt have no God before me"), but also incites them to tear down the altars of other gods, break their pillars, and cut down their sacred poles. In truth, the Greek translation used by Josephus had altered the meaning of the original Hebrew text, which sounds more like "don't curse the divine."[3] It is also likely that both the word choice of the Greek translator and Josephus's decision to promote it were determined by the need to make a compromise with the polytheistic world they lived in. But this is not the most interesting point.

In my opinion it is more worth paying attention to the specific explanation given by Josephus to his readers—and probably to himself as well—about this attitude of openness toward other gods that he claims was expressed by the Legislator. The respect he speaks of is not directed toward "the gods venerated by other peoples," but rather to the Greek *noun* used to designate them: the "name of god," *theós,* the same word used by Josephus to name *his* God. As a result, blaspheming, ridiculing, or speaking badly about the *theói,* and thus bringing the noun *theós* into disrespectful utterances or contexts, means touching *one's own* God with the stain of blasphemy or derision. The respect that Josephus professes toward the gods of others boils down basically to a purely *linguistic* phenomenon. Philo (first century CE), who also invoked this rule from the Septuagint translation of Exodus, was even more explicit in limiting the range of action to the verbal sphere alone. In his view, the commandment would have been proclaimed

> in order that no one of the disciples of Moses may ever become accustomed at all to treat the appellation 'god' with disrespect; for that name is always worthy of the highest respect and love.[4]

What needs to be shielded from insult, then, are not the *theói* as such, but the names designating them: the noun by which, when speaking Greek, a Jew indicates both the gods of other people and his own (the only) God. By distinguishing the referent from the word, the object from its designation, one manages to conveniently profess respect for the gods of others without having to recognize any effective divine nature—it is a question of names, not of substance.[5]

If we have chosen to point out these ancient subtleties, it is not to admire the mental agility of the authors, but because this "playing" with the *name* of god—using it in different occasions both as a generic name ("the god" or "the gods") and as a specific name to indicate a particular god, one's own—introduces us to a linguistic and particularly cultural problem of great interest insofar as it is intimately connected to the principle of exclusive uniqueness defining monotheistic religions: they use the common noun when referring to their god instead of assigning him a proper name.

While in Rome the gods were called Jupiter, Juno, or Mars—exactly how in a human context a person might be called Velleius, Gaia, or Marcus—in monotheistic religions, god is called "God," "the God."[6] From a linguistic point of view, he thus occupies an ambiguous position: he has a name that designates him both as himself as an individual figure (for instance, "God" as "the God of Christian worship"), and as a member of a particular group ("divine beings"). The root of this ambiguity was perfectly explained by the apologist Marcus Minucius Felix as early as between the second and third centuries CE:

> Neither must you ask a name for God, god is His name [*nec "Deo" nomen quaeras, "deus" nomen est*]. We have need of names when a multitude is to be separated into individuals by the special characteristics of names; to God (*Deus*), who is alone, the name god (*deus*) is the whole.[7]

Given that the being called "god" is the sole member of the entire group (there are, no other "gods" but him, not even linguistically), there's no need to find a proper name to indicate him: the common noun is enough. But by reasoning this way we find ourselves in front of one of the most singular paradoxes caused by the exclusive uniqueness of the god of monotheisms. Considering that both in Christianity and in Islam, the divinity bears the name of "God," it would seem obvious to arrive at the conclusion that both of these religions must worship, for all intents and purposes, the same god. On the contrary, though, both sides have a hard time admitting that the divinity called by the Muslims Allah, that is "the God," is the same as the one called by the Christians "God," even if they both have been given the same name. Although the most illuminated or open-minded believers could possibly imagine an identity of the two gods, that doesn't mean there is any shortage of quite opposite opinions negating any equation between the Christian God and Allah. This conceptual conflict continues to be a part of the contemporary world,[8] and the reason is obvious: the unique and exclusive nature of God makes the common noun take on the status of a "proper" name to such an extent that it cannot find any equivalent term outside of the common linguistic code of its worshipers. And yet, within a group that speaks multiple languages but shares the same religious background, the name of God should be perfectly "translatable": just think of the Latin *Deus* (from which derives the Italian "Dio"), then the English

"God," the Greek "Θεός," the Russian "Бог," and so on. The reason for this possibility is clear: so long as we are certain that "our" God is the only one, and the same one for everyone else, we can confidently use different terms to refer to him when we pass from one language to another.

The untranslatability of the name of God has its clearest, or at least most famous, example in what took place during the first half of the seventeenth century in the so-called "Chinese Rites Controversy," the fulcrum of which was precisely the "translation" of the name of God. During his missionary work in China, the Italian Jesuit Matteo Ricci and his successors were forced by circumstance to propose a version of Christianity using words and notions colored by local culture and traditions in order to make it more easily accessible to the intellectual world in which they were operating. As a result, the Christian God was termed *Tian* (Sky), *Shangdi* (King of the Heights), *Tianzhu* (Lord of the Sky). But these policies of "accommodation" initiated by Father Ricci and further carried out by his successors elicited a number of criticisms and censorious interventions by traditionalist enemies, to which the Jesuits faithful to Ricci's model replied in an equally decisive manner. The *querelle* would end with no less than the suicide of Father Trigault, who felt himself incapable of defending the accuracy of the term *Shangdi* to his liking.

The accusation against these translations of the name of God was that they left an opening to idolatry insofar as the chosen Chinese terms were not deemed sufficiently free of local religious implications to be used for the God of Christianity. From our point of view, though, the most interesting aspect is the following. The opponents of Ricci's model proposed the idea that the name of "God" be rendered through three Chinese ideograms that, phonetically, made a sound similar to the Latin *Deus*.

This was the same method used by missionaries in Japan, explaining Catholic doctrine by applying terms not borrowed from the local language, but by introducing Latin and Portuguese words, in particular making use of the Latin *Deus* in order to indicate the God they were preaching about.[9] Minucius Felix had taught it clearly, *nec "deo" nomen quaeras, "deus" nomen est:* neither must you ask a name for God, god is His name. As a consequence, the noun *deus* acts as a common noun that, at the same time, has taken on the role of a proper name; indeed, of an absolute proper name, if that can be said. But this is an inevitably contradictory situation: God is designated by an appellation that is simultaneously translatable (as a common noun) and untranslatable (as a proper name).

The paradox of the untranslatability of the name of "God" becomes even more apparent when this linguistic impasse is contrasted with what happens in ancient polytheisms, as we saw above. In Rome Iuppiter is the translation of *Zéus,* Iuno stands for *Héra,* and so forth, in the sense that these divinities can be co-identified simply by giving the name of one to the other. And yet each of these, within its own religious system, is distinguished by a different *proper* name, not a *common* noun. But the entity known simply by the common noun of "god" in monotheisms cannot be translated by another word, even if that word means "god" in the linguistic code of a different religion. It would be as if we easily accepted replacing "Paul" with a completely different name such as "Otto," or "Mary" with "Geneviève," but then refused to translate "man" as "uomo" or "spirit" as "esprit." The unique and exclusive configuration of the divine, as it is conceived within the monotheistic religions, has thus had the power to influence grammar itself and to confound even its most basic rules, creating a short circuit between the categories of "proper names" and "common nouns." It's enough to recall Joseph Justus Scaliger (the great philologist of the second half of the sixteenth century who had his own personal experience with religious disputes), in particular his annotation under the heading "Grammatica:"

> Would I were a good grammarian: that is the one essential for a sound understanding of all the authors. Whoever call men of any learning 'mere grammarians,' are themselves invariably utter dunces. Ignorance of grammar is the one source of dissent in religion.[10]

CHAPTER EIGHT

The *Interpretatio* of the Gods

Tacitus' *Germania* is an invaluable ethnographic work on the practices and customs of northern European peoples. In a short passage in chapter 43 the author describes some of the gods of the Nahanarvali, a people about whom admittedly little is known:

> Among these last is shown a grove of immemorial sanctity. A priest in female attire has the charge of it. But the deities are described in Roman interpretation [*interpretatio romana*] as Castor and Pollux. Such, indeed, are the attributes of the divinities, the name being Alcis. They have no images, or, indeed, any vestige of foreign superstition, but it is as brothers and as youths that the deities are worshiped.

According to Tacitus the gods called Alci by the Nahanarvali are presented as if they were Castor and Pollux. While describing the relationship established between the Germanic gods and the Roman ones, the historian uses a term that seems to evoke the act of translation: *interpretatio*. So, Castor and Pollux would be the "Roman translation" of the mysterious Germanic Alci, and vice versa? As can easily be imagined, this question is of great interest to my argument. I would like to take a closer look at what is going on here.

In truth, the word *interpretatio* means something different, and at the same time something more than simply "translation." In Latin, *interpretatio* is used to indicate the *interpretive mediation* established, in general, between a specific utterance on one side and a receiver on the other—a mediation that may consist in a translation in our sense; but it is more than that. In proper terms the act of *interpretatio* corresponds to the work carried out by an *interpres,* a mediator of an *economic* nature; as the etymology of the word tells us, the *interpres* is originally the person who holds an intermediate position "between" (*inter-*) two parties, and as such is allowed to set the *pretium* "price" (*-pres*) relative to an unresolved business affair.[1] In other words, the meaning of *interpretatio* is found within the sphere of negotiation and compromise. Consequently, giving an *interpretatio* of a specific utterance means specifically to propose a compromise, a mediation, between the utterance and its receiver. Under normal circumstances the situation works as follows. The receiver finds himself faced with a "difficult utterance," hard to understand, which is why someone has to offer him an "easier" one, able to express the meaning in a clearer way. This easier utterance provides an *interpretatio* for the first utterance as a compromise between two parties that were struggling, so to speak, to understand each other. This is the case of the *grammaticus* who writes the *interpretatio* of a poetic text, providing paraphrases and comments; or of the *hariolus,* the soothsayer, who provides the *interpretation* of a dream, revealing its hidden meaning; or of the *augur,* who provides the *interpretation* of the "signs" sent by the gods; and so forth. One could even add to this list the case when the difficult utterance, as I have called it, is not a verse of a poem or a problematic dream, but a word, a god, or an institution of a foreign language. Only in this last case does the *interpretatio* correspond to our idea of "translation."[2] In the *Germania,* then, Tacitus does not mean to say that Castor and Pollux are the "translation" of the Alci, but that these Roman gods provide an *interpretatio* of them meant to explain, to make understandable the "difficult utterance" represented by these unknown gods.

At this point, though, I must point out a defining characteristic of *interpretatio,* intrinsic to its use: its hypothetical nature. Every *interpretatio* presupposes a level of uncertainty and arbitrariness, like when the *hariolus*/"soothsayer" hazards an *interpretatio* of a dream, only to be contradicted by events, as often happens. The *interpretatio* is a compromise, and as such leaves the door open to other possible solutions. Tacitus himself, after all, demonstrates that he knows full well that when one is trying to establish similarities between gods belonging to different cultures, the process one uses is conjectural. This is how he recalls the "interpretations" given of the Egyptian god Serapis:

> The God [Serapis] himself, because he heals the sick, many identified with Æsculapius; others with Osiris, the deity of the highest antiquity among these nations; not a few with Jupiter, as being supreme ruler of all things; but most people with Pluto, arguing from the emblems which may be seen on his statues, or from tortuous conjectures [*per ambages coniectant*] of their own.[3]

In order to establish corresponding identities between gods of different cultures, then, one must proceed by hypothetical steps. In formulating them, one builds upon a foundation of single aspects found in the foreign god that match up with the characteristics of "our" gods, or at least of other known gods: their sphere of influence (medicine = Asclepius), religious tradition (ancient god of those lands = Osiris), their power (absolute lordship = Jupiter), the typical characteristics of the gods (exhibited attributes = Pluto), and finally, the "tortuous conjectures" that Tacitus does not even deem worthy of explicit mention. The verb used by Tacitus, *coniectant,* leaves no room for doubt: whoever identifies Serapis with Pluto does so by *conjecturing.* This is not the place to follow this line of reasoning any further; it is sufficient to add that when ancient authors, Roman and Greek alike, wanted to establish relationships of analogy or identification between a foreign god and one of their own, they were regularly operating in the sphere of conjecture.[4] The only certainty is the following: correspondences between the two pantheons *are possible,* but which of "our" gods were to be paired up with the foreign ones is a matter of conjecture and debate.

If we have chosen to take our readers on this brief voyage through the intricacies of Latin texts, it is not merely in order to have a better understanding of the word *interpretatio.* My argument is not limited to philology or to the history of ancient religions. What has been stated serves the purpose primarily of showing an important aspect of how ancient cultures understood their relationship with foreign gods, the *experimental* nature that often accompanied these associations. It is not simply a matter of translating one god into another (as if you could just plug them into Google Translator), but of observing, researching, and debating in order to come up with an interpretation that was not without its ambiguities, and against which you could always juxtapose or counterpose another. This idea of the divine is in flux, I might say, and has its roots in the flexibility inherent to a polytheistic system, in its intrinsically open and creative nature, which is such an important aspect of it. I will return to this in a moment; for now, I want to point out how this flexibility was so strong that the practice of *interpretatio* was not utilized just for foreign gods, but even for their own. Along these lines I can posit a genuine "intralingual *interpretatio*" of gods built along the lines of the "intralingual translation" evoked by Roman Jakobson with regards to the paraphrasing or rewriting of a specific utterance within a single language.[5]

The polemical writings of Arnobius can help us see this phenomenon more clearly. The Christian apologist observes in a passage from *Adversus Nationes* how many believe that the Earth, which provides food for all living creatures, is Cybele, while others think that it is Ceres, for she is the seed bearer, and still others believe it is Vesta, because she is the only being at rest in the entire universe. He continues:

> Now if this is propounded and maintained on sure grounds in like manner, on your interpretation (*vobis interpretibus*), three deities have no existence: neither Ceres nor Vesta are to be reckoned in the number of the gods; nor, in fine, can the mother of the gods herself, whom Nigidius thinks to have been married to Saturn, be rightly declared a goddess, if indeed these are all names of the one earth, and it alone is signified by these titles.[6]

The paradox of Arnobius reveals an important aspect of ancient religiosity: the possibility to interpret—amongst themselves—gods from the same pantheon by establishing reciprocal relationships of association among them. The mechanism of *interpretatio* thus works not only with the gods of other peoples, projected *externally*, but also *internally*. The tools remain the same: evaluating some of the identifying features of each god (source of food, bearer of seeds, stability) in order to draw inferences that produce an association with another god, just as Serapis is identified as Asclepius, Osiris, or Jupiter, based on the different aspects of the god. Except that within the same culture the game is being played on only half of a field and with only the players of a single team. The rules, though, are the same.

CHAPTER NINE

Polytheism, Curiosity, and Knowledge

After showing how the classical polytheistic religions behaved in terms of their relationship with the gods of others, I would like to address which of these aspects most surprises us, the heirs (more or less consciously) of monotheism.

Certainly, the capacity to associate different gods from different religions and cultures as to establish a relationship of reciprocal interpretation between them is unexpected, while the Mosaic distinction makes such a process practically inconceivable. If you start from the premise that your god is the only true god—while the gods of others are either false gods or demon creatures—it is obvious that you cannot "interpret" your exclusive god as another god taken from different peoples and cultures. This remains true even (or perhaps especially) when the gods in question share qualities that could support an initial hypothesis upon which to base this association. The fundamental difference between polytheisms and monotheisms must not be underestimated. Precisely this attitude forms the cornerstone of one of the most astonishing phenomena of civilizations of classical antiquity when compared to those born after the advent of monotheism. I am speaking of the previously mentioned fact that even though violence was certainly a reality among these societies, religious conflicts and wars were essentially not a factor in this violence. The reason for this remarkable situation now becomes clearer. On the one hand, as previously stated, the *plural* nature of the gods *per se* prevented religious conflict—if our gods are already numerous, there is no reason to negate or to fight over the existence of other people's gods. On the other hand, the possibility of actually "interpreting" a god or goddess from another culture rendered them unthreatening. At this point, religious conflict had neither a place nor a reason to exist. In polytheistic cultures, the gods of others were seen not as a menace to the unique truth of one's own god, but as an opportunity, sometimes even a resource.

What I pointed out, though, makes another cultural gap between monotheism and polytheism come to the fore. In this case the difference is played out in terms of *curiosity.* One is surprised by the interest that the ancients showed toward other gods, by their desire to know and interpret these figures in order to establish possible analogies and relationships between "ours" and "theirs." When Tacitus asks himself which Roman gods correspond to the Alci of the unknown Nahanarvali, he demonstrates above all an attentiveness and interest toward other people's divinities. Perhaps even more interesting, though, is that this attitude is not found exclusively at the level of high culture, literature, or philosophy, but also in average life. Alongside Tacitus, the ethnologist who "speculates" about the identity of two Nahanarvali deities, we find a simple soldier stationed in Germania who writes a dedication to *Mercurius Gebrinius* or *Mars HalamarΘ*, thereby associating a Roman god with a local one; or a resident of Trier who makes a dedication to *Vertumnus sive Pisintus*.[1] Knowing the gods, even those belonging to others, is an intrinsic aspect of the polytheistic concept of religion. In this light, I can once again return to the testimony of Arnobius.

In order to demonstrate how the novelty of the Christian religion neither could nor should scandalize anyone, the apologist created a list of "new" gods that the Romans had integrated into their ceremonies over time: Isis, Serapis, Cybele, Apollo himself (who, according to learned Romans, was not found on the list of gods compiled by Numa Pompilius, the second king of Rome), the Greek Ceres. And here is how the apologist expressed himself about the relationship established by the Romans with Cybele in his own days: "What! did you not begin both to know and be acquainted with [*et nosse et scire coepistis*], and to worship with remarkable honors the Phrygian mother...?"[2] The emphasis placed on the act of "knowing" a god, made quite clear by the recurrent verbs of *nosse et scire* in the text, is significant. But *coepistis*, "you have begun," which modifies both of the verbs of knowledge, is interesting too. "Knowing and understanding" a god, by this logic, starts at a precise moment in time. There is a moment in which "one learns" about a certain god and recognizes his or her traits, after which the related ceremonies can even be officially approved (when considered suitable). Arnobius pushes the point even further:

> Now it is clear and manifest from this, that he [Apollo], too, was unknown [*incognitum*] to you, but that at some time afterwards he began to be known also [*coepisse esse ... notum*]. If anyone, therefore, should ask you why you have so lately begun to worship those deities whom we mentioned just now, it is certain that you will reply [...] because we were till lately not aware [*nesciebamus*] that they were gods.[3]

The gods of others are then, as it seems, something to be "recognized" over time. Once their existence is made known (it is certainly astonishing to hear that even Apollo, god of the Palatine Hill, could have remained unknown to the Romans for such a long time), one can undertake the process of integrating them into one's own set of gods.[4] This process, therefore, demonstrates interest, curiosity, and the desire to "know" the gods of others. On the other hand, with the exception of the attitudes of more open-minded or illuminated people, the monotheistic domain reveals no such curiosity or desire to know other gods; rather, a feeling of indifference or superiority, if not outright hostility, is more likely. Jordan Paper, an anthropologist who has dedicated decades of his life to the study of Chinese and native North American religions, describes how his Chinese wife

> has experienced a half-century of her Chinese religious understanding being attacked by Christian missionaries, American politicians, and even ordinary Westerners as essentially wrong. And she is well aware that this has been going on for over five centuries.[5]

These attacks are a consequence of a cult of only one God directly linked to the conviction that he is also the only *true* god: beyond him there is nothing but falsehood. For what possible reason should someone who believes himself to be on the side of truth feel curiosity or interest, instead of indifference or even repulsion, toward what is false? Along these lines, it is worthwhile to recall that it was precisely this "curiosity" toward the divine that was harshly reprimanded by Tertullian (between the second and third centuries CE) who wrote, "We want no curious disputation [*curiositas*] after possessing Christ Jesus, no inquisition after enjoying the gospel! ... Let such curious art give place to faith.... To know nothing in opposition to the rule of faith, is to know all things."[6]

At this point, I think I am ready to make another comparison between the ways of thinking of polytheism and monotheism. As is well known, one of the most pressing needs of today's world, not only for religious peace but for peace in general, is interfaith dialogue: a form of discussion and exchange that keeps religions from becoming frozen in their own viewpoints and allows them to remain open to mutual contact and availability. This impulse is not inspired only by the desire to heal the wounds of the past, but also by the hope to forestall present and future conflicts in a world where globalism seems to motivate always more emphatically identitarian sectarianism, including religious sectarianism.[7] The urgency of a need for dialogue is documented by the hundreds of books in various languages dedicated to this topic (any respectable library has many shelves of them), not to mention the numerous initiatives carried out, with greater or lesser success, on this score.[8] I would like to try to observe, though, the practice or the intentions of interfaith dialogue through polytheistic eyes. The difference is clear. On one hand you have the often unsuccessful desire, good will, projects, and attempts to establish a dialogue between religions with difficulties in finding common ground;[9] on the other, you find curiosity manifested toward the gods of others in the ancient world, the desire to learn about them in order to eventually make them your own. In another sense, among these two conceptions there is a gap in terms of knowledge and social distribution. I can imagine that only a few members of the elite and a limited number of culturally and ethically progressive groups are able to understand the importance of interfaith dialogue, while a majority of believers or semi-believers not only show no interest in other religions but probably find out of place or barely legitimate the curiosity of others.[10] On the contrary, the attention paid by the ancients to the gods of others was a widespread phenomenon, as has been shown, both in the intellectual forms chosen by historians and philosophers, and in the practical, daily forms of commoners. From this perspective, then, there can be no question that re-activating this repressed polytheistic potential (curiosity toward the gods of others), so closely connected to the practice of *interpretatio* between foreign gods, would greatly simplify matters.

CHAPTER TEN

What If Monotheisms Were Just Polytheisms in Disguise?

The central importance of the concept of interpretation, as we have seen it at work within polytheistic cultures, allows me to freshly examine an oft-repeated truism about the three great monotheistic religions. We are talking about the fact that other divine beings—angels, devils, demons, saints, the Virgin Mary, or better yet the various Virgin Marys—can be found alongside the one God, which would seem to make Christian monotheism nothing more than a polytheism in disguise. This remark was frequently aimed at Christianity from at least the beginning of the third century on, and was often formulated as an accusation.[1]

It is simple to demonstrate that more commonalities exist between ancient polytheisms and contemporary monotheisms than one might like to find. Even the configuration of the Christian divine into the form of the Trinity, in all of its diverse theological formulations, bends the idea of the uniqueness of God toward a plurality of "persons." Looking more closely within the structure of Catholicism, I should mention how the powers of individual saints were assigned on the basis of their various spheres of intervention (St. Rocco = dog bites, St. Lucy = sight, St. Venantius = falls), just as the Romans entrusted diverse *officia,* or "tasks," to their gods (Lucina = birth, Janus = beginnings, Bellona = war). In their roles as patron of cities (St. Januarius, Naples; St. Peter, Rome), saints functioned similarly to the ancient *poliádes* ("of the city") divinities, the gods or goddesses providing special protection to a given city (Hera, Argos; Artemis, Ephesus). Therefore a protective function can be carried out by the Virgin Mary, as is well known, when she is invoked as the guardian of regions, cities, or nations. Furthermore, this does not take into account that through her countless specifications (Madonna of Perpetual Succour, of Pilar, of Pompeii), this divine figure brings the ancient mechanism of the *epíklesis* back to life, a mechanism by which a single divine power could have various representations (Juno Regina, Juno Lanuvina), all the while retaining her unique self.[2]

In my opinion, though, the difference between monotheism and polytheism is not to be found merely in the fact that in the former, there is only a single divine entity in the "class of deity," while in the latter there are many.[3] The true distance between the more apparently polytheistic variants of monotheism and "real" polytheism can be found, once again, in the possibility or impossibility of interpretation. As much as Catholic monotheism can refract into a multitude of saints, the idea of "interpreting" one of these as a similar being, such as an angel or djinn from a different monotheistic religious universe or even a divinity belonging to some polytheistic pantheons, can never be considered legitimate. The polytheistic monotheisms, if we choose to qualify them as such, operate constantly and exclusively *within* their own religious horizon: just as it is not allowed to interpret one's own unique god with a god that belongs to another religion, it is not even permitted to interpret a saint or a Virgin Mary with a supernatural being belonging to a different pantheon. The uniqueness and exclusivity of God extends through the panoply of the other supernatural figures surrounding him, making their own plurality equally exclusive. If we admit, then, that the monotheisms here discussed can be considered polytheisms in disguise, we should not ignore the fact that these are still, nonetheless, "exclusive polytheisms," still defined by the original Mosaic distinction. Independently from the number of divine entities in play, the distinctive characteristic of monotheism lies always in the impossibility of *interpretatio*.

CHAPTER ELEVEN

Tolerance vs. *Interpretatio*

Let me go back to where my story began. As you will recall, when in the opening chapter of this book I spoke about the sacrifice of the nativity scene and the threats to destroy the mosque in Colle Val d'Elsa, I resorted to the notion of "tolerance." This word "tolerance," still widely in use in our cultural debates, usually means "sympathy or indulgence for beliefs or practices differing from or conflicting with one's own."[1] In this regard, I argued how the teachers who supported the removal of nativity scenes had shown extreme religious tolerance, while an equally extreme religious intolerance had been displayed by those people who wanted to blow up the minaret. But where does this term "tolerance" come from? Let me briefly examine its birth and early meaning.

Tolerantia is a Latin word related to the verb *tolero,* "to bear," and it means precisely the practice of enduring something, better known as patience. Among the non-Christian Roman authors, *tolerantia* was a virtue, but a personal one, not a social one. *Tolerantia* was practiced facing an adverse situation or suffering (patiently enduring *incommoda,* "discomfort"; *dolor,* "pain";

or *dura et aspera*, "harsh and difficult conditions"), or as one could say, those *res humanae* or "human facts" to which people are inevitably subjected. The wise man instead faced adversity through the soul's strength, "protected by the walls of virtues," the most important of which is *tolerantia*.[2] Similarly, we are forced or asked to *tolerare* things like fatigue, the harshness of military life, and the *violentia* "violence" of fate, such as excessive severity or an insult we receive.[3] It is only after the advent of Christian authors, and St. Augustine in particular, that *tolerantia* and *tolerare* would make their entrance within the realm of social ethics, especially with regards to religious diversity. Whereas Cyprian had spoken about Jesus as having been able to "tolerate the Judaeans" (*in Iudaeis tolerandis*), Augustine would expressly invite to practice *tolerantia* when dealing with those who "think differently (*diversa sentientes*)" within Christianity, by which he meant the heretics. If we may borrow a phrase from the Baron d'Holbach, we are at the stage in which "God becomes interested in the opinions of men."[4] Augustine's position is the following: we must "tolerate the evildoers who bring about schism" (*ad tolerandos in schismate malos*)—taking inspiration from Paul ("one who endures false brothers," *falsorum fratrum tolerator*)—in order to remain united with them. This behavior on the one hand recalls charity, the virtue most characteristic of Christians, and on the other opportunism: to behave otherwise would in fact put the primary asset of the Church—its unity—at risk. It is preferable to "endure" rather than react. Do note, however, that as far as the relationship with pagans and Judaeans is concerned, Augustine never uses terms like *tolerantia* or *tolerare*.[5]

As one can see, tolerance is born within a strongly limiting context. On one side it requires endurance and not acceptance or recognition of what must be indeed tolerated; on the other, it also assumes that the object to be tolerated is something negative (the *mali* of Augustine, the evildoers). Let us not forget, then, that *tolerantia* is practiced within a context that encourages tolerance and its exercise, but which does not remotely question the absolute and intrinsic *truth* of one's own religious ideas: those who think differently do not simply have different opinions, but they are wrong, even sinfully wrong. They are heretics. Consequently, the resort to *tolerantia* is motivated on the basis of arguments that exclude different ideas as well as the people who profess them regardless of their intrinsic legitimacy. Ideas and people are indeed "tolerated" not because these ideas or these people deserve any distinction per se, but out of the general principle of charity or in consideration of the wellbeing of the Church, or for both reasons at once. However, charity has its limits, just as the welfare and the advantage of the Church may at some point no longer feel the need to tolerate *diversa sentientes* and may choose to resort to harsher, more decisive actions. Indeed Augustine himself felt no qualms in his approval of the repression of the Donatists, citing various justifications spanning from the legitimate limitations of "being good" to the *compelle intrare* "compel to enter" of the Gospel parable.[6] When called upon to rein in disputes, after all, the virtue of *tolerantia* always runs the risk of letting conflict out of its cage.

The notion of tolerance would take on growing importance in the modern era against the backdrop of a Europe torn apart by conflicts between different churches and Christian sects. Through the works of Sébastien Castellion, Roger Williams, Baruch Spinoza, or Pierre Bayle[7]—and thanks to John Locke's "toleration" and Voltaire's "tolérance"—the Augustinian model of *tolerantia* would eventually evolve into our "tolerance": the term by which we designate the previously mentioned definition of "sympathy or indulgence for beliefs or practices differing from or conflicting with one's own." It's obvious that this idea still forms a fundamental principle for civil coexistence, now more than ever.[8] Nonetheless, something ambiguous remains in the concept of "tolerance" because we cannot overlook the intrinsic meaning of the word ("tolerate") or the cultural context within which it was born. As Karl Schreiner wrote, "the history of this concept is clearly marked by the tension between passive patience and active tolerance, between the capability of bearing evil and the recognition of the other in his own effective otherness. The lack of unambiguity has produced the result that the notion of 'tolerance' can be seen as 'spongy.'"[9] Because of these internal contradictions, religious tolerance represents a principle as desirable as it is fragile, and liable to be turned upside down. Religious tolerance does not mean a complete legitimization of the opinions of others, but implicates some kind of "disapproval" of them (if not directly of those who profess them), although always accompanied by intentionally peaceful behavior.[10] Take for example a passage previously examined in the *Catechism of the Catholic Church,* where it is stated that:

> "Nobody may be forced to act against his convictions, nor is anyone to be restrained from acting in accordance with his conscience in religious matters in private or in public, alone or in association with others, within due limits." This right is based on the very nature of the human person, whose dignity enables him freely to assent to the divine truth which transcends the temporal order. For this reason it "continues to exist even in those who do not live up to their obligation of seeking the truth and adhering to it."[11]

This text clearly shows the inherent contradictions found within the principle of religious tolerance. On one side, there is the declaration according to which no one can be forced to adhere to another faith or be prohibited from practicing his own. On the other, it reiterates that a person makes a mistake in refusing to accept certain religious principles, a mistake that in truth one would be "obliged" to correct by seeking the "truth." It is easy to imagine how, when played out against the backdrop of a different political and philosophical context, this contrast between those who seek the truth and those who *do not* could easily lead to situations and behaviors that might well be defined as "intolerant."

Let me return now to polytheistic terrain. I would like to place the modern concept of religious tolerance "back to back"—in the comparative spirit of de Tocqueville[12]—with the ancient polytheistic concept of *interpretatio* analyzed in the previous chapters. One detail immediately comes to mind: in a culture that does not expect God to be an exclusive, unique deity and where the possibility exists of interpreting the gods of others as your own, an idea such as religious tolerance finds itself, at the very least, out of place.[13] There is no reason to "tolerate" those who pay homage to a god who is different from mine when I have the capacity to assimilate or even identify this god with one I already know and worship. Let me try, rather, to reexamine the relevant attributes of ancient polytheistic systems already highlighted when analyzing the implications of *interpretatio* of foreign gods: an absence of religiously motivated wars, the tendency to experiment with the divine, curiosity and the habit of getting to know about foreign gods, the use of intralingual *interpretatio.* Religious tolerance, as defined here, is able to put into practice this collection of characteristics only partially. In other words, the behavior of someone who shows "sympathy or indulgence for beliefs or practices differing from or conflicting with one's own," even in matters of religion, feels like a cultural construct destined to wane precisely because of the *lack* of what a polytheistic *interpretatio* offers by its very nature. It is as if when applying the principle of tolerance, each and every feature that we have identified is reproduced in a weakened form. The endogenous absence of religious conflicts is scaled down to a commitment (regularly placed under strain) not to trigger anymore; the tendency to experiment with the divine pantheon of others shrinks into not forbidding the freedom of religious expression; curiosity and the habit of "getting to know" foreign gods hides behind a screen of simple respect (as happened with the sacrifice of the nativity scene). And as for intralingual *interpretatio*—i.e., the possibility to interpret gods from the same pantheon, establishing reciprocal associations among them—in my opinion it was exactly the absence of this resource that produced, in the end, the birth of tolerance in Europe. For centuries the various Christian churches and sects proved unable to "interpret" their differing representations of the divine and as a result set off countless bloody wars *despite* the fact that they all practiced the same religion. The concept of "tolerance" for the religious beliefs and practices of others emerged to manage these impossibilities.

CHAPTER TWELVE

Polytheism as Language

I will now return to the "translation" or "translatability" of the gods as presented by Jan Assmann. Clearly, this way of describing the assimilation of different deities implies the use of a concept taken from the field of *linguistics*. In other words, in order to explain the polytheistic strategies enacted between gods belonging to different religions, I can establish an analogy with what happens between foreign languages, where one word is translatable into another. The possibility of using a linguistic category to describe what takes place in the field of ancient religions is cause for great interest, and may prove quite useful. It is a fair question to ask ourselves whether ancient polytheism in fact practiced not only the translation of gods, but also other linguistic functions[1]

If I take up this hypothesis, one of the first functions that comes to mind is precisely what we called "intralingual *interpretatio*," the possibility of translating one god into another even within the same pantheon. In linguistic terms this process finds a parallel every time we try to clarify or rephrase something that we have already said, "interpreting" a given lexeme or enunciation through other words coming from the same language. Furthermore, the continuous process of divine *proliferation* within polytheistic systems greatly resembles the process by which the vocabulary of a language grows over time, adding on words that previously did not exist. This was the case in Rome with gods and goddesses such as Honos, Fides, Mens, and Concordia, gods that were "produced" over the passage of time. Or even, as Cicero himself noticed, when the pantheon grew through the process of divinization of mortals such as Hercules or Asclepius.[2] Inversely, gods and goddesses can fall into disuse over the years, as happened for example in Rome with the goddess Vacuna, whose identification became problematic (leading to multiple, all uncertain, interpretations about this divinity).[3]

This same phenomenon happens with archaic or obsolete terms within a given language of which only certain specialists or well-read people know the meaning (what, for example, does the word "mephitic" mean?). From a similar outlook of proliferation and flexibility I would like to call attention again to the process by which it is possible to juxtapose gods who originally were separate entities but who share a common quality of divine actions within a polytheistic system, thereby creating what in linguistics would be considered a "privileged syntagma," a combination between two words that, although coming from distinct norms of usage, tend to attract one another in a particular way in certain contexts ("hammer and sickle" in ideological contexts, "bread and butter" when talking about work). This is the case in the field of religion with the example of "Juno Lucina," where two distinct goddesses became associated in a single syntagma due to their connection to childbirth; the same thing happened in the same situation in Greece, producing "Artemis Eileithyia."[4]

We could keep playing this game, if we want to call it such, of linguistic representation of polytheism for a long time, but rather than provide further analogies, I prefer to focus on a particular aspect just as relevant as the one I began with. I can state not only that the ancients undertook the practice of *translating* the gods of others, as indicated by Assmann, but also of *borrowing* them, just as foreign words can be both translated and specifically integrated (borrowed) into a system that is different from its origins. As we all know, a word can move from one language to another either while maintaining its original meaning ("cocktail" means "cocktail" no matter where you use it in the world), or by undergoing a process of semantic adaptation (like the transformation of the English "beefsteak" into the Italian "bistecca," which can be used equally for a steak or for a pork chop). Similarly, polytheistic religious systems can direct their attention and interests toward the gods of others either to directly import the foreign deity into their own pantheon (as happened in Rome with gods like the Anatolian Cybele or the Greek Asklépios), or to subject them to more or less reasonable modifications, as was the case in Rome with Hercules..[5]

Remaining for a moment within this category of "borrowing," a particularly interesting example can be found in a practice that the Romans called *evocatio*. When they put a city under siege the Roman commander was given the power to "call out" (evoke, *evocatio*) the divine guardians, as took place in 396 BCE by Marcus Furius Camillus under the walls of Veii, and in 146 BCE by Publius Cornelius Scipio Africanus under the walls of Carthage. The ceremony, held with a rather complex ritual, consisted in "calling the patron gods out" of the besieged city, promising them that they would receive equal or even superior honors in Rome than they did from the enemy. In such a way, the city would lose its divine protection and would fall more easily, while in Rome, a new god would find a home. In this regard, however, it is interesting to mention what two ancient scholars, Servius and Macrobius, had to say about the motivations behind this religious practice:

> Before conquering the city, the gods were "called out" (*evocabantur*) by the enemies in order to avoid sacrilege [because] it was considered a greatly impious act (*nefas*) to take the gods prisoner.[6]

This snippet of information seems as illuminating as it is short. In moments of battle, allowing for the gods to become involved in the fall of an enemy city or to be taken prisoner, as if they were no different from the defeated citizens, was seen as a *sacrilegium* or even *nefas:* an impious act that no *mos* or "custom" could possibly justify, insofar as it violated norms of a higher order than the ordinary one.[7] One of the most ancient Roman historians, Lucius Cincius Alimentus, tells us about the actions the Romans took with regards to the gods of fallen cities in general:

> As far as the religious objects of the conquered cities were concerned, the Romans usually distributed a portion of them privately to various families, and publicly consecrated another portion; and in order to avoid leaving out any of the gods, either because of their multitude or out of ignorance, they were all invoked collectively through a single name, *Novensiles,* for the sake of synthesis and brevity.[8]

Even when the gods of others were not merely foreign gods but actual enemy gods, they were nevertheless treated with respect. The Romans did their best to ensure that their ceremonies continued to be carried out, privately or publicly, and they made efforts to make sure that they didn't fall into disuse.

I will close this section by proposing a rapid comparison between polytheistic and monotheistic ways of thinking in terms of the various "linguistic" possibilities offered by polytheistic systems: translation or translatability, the intralingual *interpretatio*, the ability to produce new divine lexemes, the creation of privileged syntagma, and especially the habit of borrowing from the world of foreign gods. As previously shown, such *possibilities* represent an equal number of *impossibilities* for monotheistic religions. The absolute condition of a single true god gives these religions a rigid language within which it is impossible not only to translate one's own god into another foreign god, but even to move toward an intralingual *interpretatio* within one's own system; or worse: trying to do so runs the risk of leading into heresy, as in the truly emblematic case of the trinitary controversy, which generated numerous different "intralingual interpretations" among the Father, the Son, and the Holy Ghost, all of which gave rise to conflicts. Similarly, for monotheisms it is impossible to create new divine lexemes or to enrich the heritage of the existing gods through the creation or adoption of new ones. This is an impossibility that Nietzsche, in his anti-monotheistic and anti-Christian ardor, expressly decried: "Two thousand years have come and gone—and not a single new god!"[9] This monotheistic lexical rigidity finds a partial exception in Catholicism, which shows certain parallels with polytheism in the following way. The beatification or sanctification of new persons by the Church represents a testimony of proliferation within this religion, comparable to the adoption of new gods in ancient religions. However, this Catholic practice—rejected by other versions of Christianity—regards only what we could call a subordinate, if not inferior, level of the spiritual world.

The most interesting aspect of the comparison, though, is represented by what I have called the borrowing of gods, an unacceptable practice for monotheisms for the same reason that they cannot even conceive of the translatability of gods.[10] The two phenomena derive from a single structural impossibility, dictated by the unique and exclusive characteristic of their god. In particular, looking again at the practice of *evocatio* as described above, the most striking aspect from a comparative point of view is the claim that the Romans would do this in order "to avoid sacrilege" by committing "a great impiety (*nefas*) by taking the gods prisoner." This is not merely a reflection of the fact that religious conflicts were fundamentally absent in the ancient polytheistic world. There is more going on here: when conflicts did arise for whatever reason, efforts were made to keep the gods out of it. With this in mind, I would like to mention once again the commandment in Exodus—"You shall tear down their altars, break their pillars, and cut down their sacred poles (for you shall worship no other god, because the Lord, whose name is Jealous, is a jealous God)"[11]—in order to understand another important difference between religious thought inspired by polytheism and religious thought governed by religions of the single god. These are two diametrically opposed and inverse attitudes: what you *should not* do in a polytheistic context is precisely what you *should* do in monotheism. There are, sadly, far too many examples of this in our history, both past and present, such as the threats of aggression against the mosque in Colle Val d'Elsa, or the real, bloody attacks on Christian churches in Egypt and elsewhere.

CHAPTER THIRTEEN

Giving Citizenship to the Gods

How did ancient Rome understand borrowing and receiving foreign gods? There is very interesting evidence related to this topic, and even a brief exploration of it will allow me to establish an important point and avoid the possibility of a misunderstanding.

If it was truly possible to accept other gods as one's own within ancient religions, this did not mean that a new god would automatically be honored and worshiped within the city, as if he or she were comparable to those of established tradition. In order to obtain full acceptance the foreign god had to first go through an official naturalization process (to borrow today's terminology) deliberated upon by the Senate, which would end with the public establishment of the god's cult.[1] Amongst the religiously motivated laws mentioned by Cicero, we find the following:

> No one should have separate gods for themselves unless they have been publicly recognized (*publice adscitos*); privately the gods that are worshiped are those that were previously worshiped by their fathers.[2]

The attitude revealed by this rule is rather strict; in order to be worshiped, the new gods—i.e., gods newly created, like the ones just mentioned,[3] or foreign ones that had been imported—must receive official recognition from the government. As for private worship, on the other hand, trust was placed in the hands of ancestral traditions. On the subject of foreign gods, even the emperor Augustus seemed to follow similar criteria to those mentioned by Cicero. His biographer Suetonius tells us:

> With regard to the religious ceremonies of foreign nations, he was a strict observer of those which had been established by ancient custom; but others he held in no esteem. For, having been initiated at Athens [into the Eleusinian mysteries], and coming afterwards to hear a cause at Rome, relative to the privileges of the priests of the Attic Ceres, when some of the mysteries of the sacred rites were to be introduced in the pleadings, he dismissed those who sat upon the bench as judges with him, as well as the by-standers, and heard the argument upon those points himself. But, on the other hand, he not only declined, in his progress through Egypt, to go out of his way to pay a visit to Apis, but he likewise commended his grandson Gaius for not paying his devotions at Jerusalem in his passage through Judea.[4]

Augustus thus showed great respect for the Attic Ceres, a foreign goddess who had officially been introduced into Rome many years earlier, but at the same time he seems to have little consideration both for Egyptian and Hebrew gods. An ancient scholar, Sextus Pompeius Festus, later explains which foreign gods were officially recognized, and how they were worshiped:

> Foreign religions (*peregrina sacra*) is the name given both to those brought to Rome by means of *evocatio* during a city-siege, and those that have been requested out of a specific religious need during times of peace, such as the worship of Cybele from Phrygia, that of

> Ceres from Greece, that of Asclepius from Epidaurus. These rituals are celebrated according to the customs whence they were adopted.[5]

But rather than pile up evidence, I am more interested here in retracing the mental path that led the Romans to accept and publicly recognize the gods. The verb usually used to indicate this process, in fact, was *adscisco,* which literally means "recognize": *publice adscitos,* as stated by the religious law reported by Cicero on the foreign gods whose worship had been publicly sanctioned, just as the worship of Attic Ceres was *adscita,* and the worship of the Phrygian Cybele was *adscita.*[6] This word, *adscisco,* is a technical term taken from the legal jargon used to indicate the act of co-opting someone; one can be *adscitus* to become a member of the Senate, or even more interestingly, with *adscisco* one can indicate the act of giving citizenship to a person, naturalizing him in one's own city. In some fashion, the foreign god, in order to be integrated within the religions of the *civitas,* had to be naturalized as a "citizen" of Rome, co-opted among its members. It does not seem even remotely accidental, then, that in order to justify the entry of a Greek word within their Latin vocabulary—what we have identified as linguistic borrowing—Roman writers relied upon the same phraseology used to describe the borrowing of a god: *verbum latina civitate donare:* "giving Latin citizenship to a word." Citizenship was given to words coming from foreign languages just as it was given to foreign gods, and in both cases the act of borrowing was represented by the same cultural phenomenon. For Romans, citizenship was not only a legal right or a political practice, but a genuine "cognitive metaphor," a way of thinking and organizing their culture.[7]

Going back to the gods, other statements by ancient authors show how the mental process that led to a god's integration was based on the same model of co-opting and of citizenship.[8] Cicero writes about Hercules, Asclepius, Castor and Pollux, and Romulus as gods "who were welcomed into the heavens almost as if they were newly recognized citizens (*quasi novos et adscripticios cives*)"; while Josephus, from his Jewish perspective, would criticize that "the orators were allowed to give citizenship, by decree, to each and every foreign god they felt was useful."[9] In truth, according to this deeply rooted way of thinking in Roman culture, gods were considered for all intents and purposes citizens, or more accurately, "fellow-citizens," members of the same *civitas,* even if they were divine. As Cicero wrote, once again in the *Laws,* "the Greeks and Romans, in order to increase *pietas* toward the gods, chose to make them residents (*incolere*), of our very own cities."[10]

Even in the imagination of poets, the divine world was organized like the social and political life of the City. Ovid did not hesitate in dividing up the houses of the gods into noble and plebeian neighborhoods, each according to their rank, as if he were describing the reality of Rome and its "human" citizens. Jupiter lived in a kind of "Palatine in the sky," and the council of gods that he convokes resembles a session of the Senate to a remarkable degree.[11] There is a fundamental principle behind all of these different examples, one that profoundly differentiates Roman religion from the one that substituted it : the conviction that the gods and their worship are a function of the human community, a consequence of them, and not the other way around. We owe it to Augustine that we possess the following extremely revelatory sentence by Marcus Terentius Varro, most likely taken from his *Antiquities of the Human and Divine Things:*

> This very same Varro testifies that he wrote first concerning human things, but afterwards concerning divine things, because the states

> (*civitates*) existed first, and afterward these things were instituted by them. [...] The following is the reason Varro gives when he confesses that he had written first concerning human things, and afterwards of divine things, because these divine things were instituted by men:—'As the painter is before the painted tablet, the mason before the edifice, so states (*civitates*) are before those things which are instituted by states.'[12]

Augustine did not agree with Varro, and it is not hard to imagine why: "But the true religion," he objected, "was not instituted by any earthly state (*civitas*).... It, however, is inspired and taught by the true God." In the eyes of someone who belonged to a culture that saw God as the creator of the universe, religion could be nothing less than an absolute prerequisite, and thus the contrary idea that it was men who instituted divine things could be no less than incomprehensible. But, with all due respect to Augustine, Romans had exactly this kind of world view: first come the *civitates,* then come the *res divinae,* which are institutions created by the *civitates,* just like a painting or an edifice is the *product* of its maker.[13]

This cultural habit—god as a function or consequence of the City—helps explain expressions at first glance surprising from a modern perspective (or to a Christian apologist). Take March 14 as an example, the day on which the *sacra* of Minerva were celebrated. On this day, according to Ovid, it was forbidden to fight and spill blood, because it was Minerva's birthday[14] Did Ovid mean that on March 14 Romans celebrated the birth of Athena from Zeus' head? Naturally, the answer is neither mythological nor theogonical.[15] The day of Minerva's birth simply corresponded with the day when the temple dedicated to her worship was officially consecrated, the *dies natalis templi.* For worshippers any given god "was born" on the day of the public ceremony consecrating the temple and authorizing the god's entrance into the City. Obviously the Christians would later make fun of this aspect of the Roman religion: "It is the birthday (*natalis*) of Tellus," Arnobius would exclaim, "for the gods are born, and have festal days on which it has been settled that they began to breathe."[16] But this is merely a way to reduce a cultural metaphor to a dull literal meaning, whereas the *dies natalis* of a god really had a rich ideological content: in Rome, a god "was born" alongside the consecration of his or her temple precisely because a god's "beginning" went hand in hand with its process of public incorporation.

This quite strange (at least for contemporary eyes) conception of the divine is confirmed yet again by Cicero in his dialogue *On the Nature of the Gods*. In this dialogue we meet Cotta, pontifex maximus and skeptic philosopher. In response to the arguments laid forth by the Stoic Balbus, Cotta says:

> No words . . . can shake me from holding the beliefs that I inherited from our forefathers, beliefs in the religion of the immortal gods. When it comes to religion, I follow the *pontifices maximi* Tiberius Coruncanius, Publius Scipio, and Publius Scaevola, and not the philosophers Zeno, Cleanthes, or Crysippus. . . . You, who are a philosopher, must give me a demonstration of religion, while I believe in our forefathers without any need of proof.[17]

In Rome, the "truth" about the gods does not come from the learned utterances of philosophy, but from the tradition established by the forefathers. For this reason, a pontifex maximus—the person who held the highest rank in the priesthoods—can allow himself not to take overly seriously the philosophical proofs placed before him about the existence of the gods. As a Roman, in fact, his point of view is first and foremost a *civic* perspective about the divine, rather than a philosophical or theological one.[18]

The conferring of citizenship onto the world of the divine in the Roman religion and the particular aspect of the public co-opting of foreign gods represent a cultural construct of great originality. Such a situation certainly required a form of state control over public religious practices (though not over private ones, as we have mentioned). As such, this would also make it impossible for just any god whatsoever to take hold of the City and impose himself as an absolute presence, or allow those who believed in him or claimed to represent him to impose their will on all citizens. Aside from this aspect, though, this civic method of establishing a foreign god's entrance "among the city" has the specific value of forcing us to rethink the importance of the concept of *citizenship*. Evidently in Rome citizenship was so crucial as to involve even the world of the gods. From this perspective, I can draw yet another line between earlier polytheistic ways of thinking and the monotheistic attitudes that would follow. Let me look again at the modern religious tolerance so arduously achieved in Europe after long and bloody years of conflict. I first made a comparison between the modern concept of tolerance and the ancient *interpretatio*, with all of its implications. I can now take the idea of tolerance and put it side by side, the way you might do with two images, not with *interpretatio* of a foreign god but with the granting of "citizenship" to a god. Once again it is easy to notice the distance between the attitude born out of Christianity and the one common to the Romans: tolerating the gods of others, even in the broadest and most positive sense of the word, is quite different from co-opting them within one's own *civitas*.

The civic way of thinking displayed by the Romans in their acceptance of the gods of others carries a symbolic value that can help us reflect upon another aspect of our contemporary lives. The last few decades have been marked by a tendency toward individualism that seems to always value a person's ethnic, cultural, linguistic, or religious identity far more than his or her civic-community identity.[19] In Italy, as in many Western nations, we are witnessing an *internal* segmentation of identity on the basis of culture, food, dialect, presumed ancestry, and other traditions, almost as if being a legal citizen of Italy were *less* important than the place where we were originally born or what kind of food we eat, either as an individual or as a group. At the same time, there has been growing tension and resistance toward immigrants, whose children are denied citizenship even when they are born within Italian borders; moreover, in the public imagination immigrants often are identified more by the religion that they practice, by their facial features, or by their (alleged) habits, than by their belonging to a common civic community. Under these conditions, Italian society finds itself between a rock and a hard place: running the risk of breaking apart into many separate communities unable to communicate amongst themselves on one side; on the other, a reactionary form of forced cultural homogenization. Only through the idea of citizenship—which guarantees legal protection for all, but demands respect of the laws from all—can we evade these two opposing tendencies.[20] This is why bringing attention to the practice of granting citizenship even to the *gods* may provide not only a precious intellectual resource, but also a social and civic resource for a society that often forgets the importance of this concept. To borrow William James's phrase once again, the god-citizens of ancient Rome today hold a great "cash-value."

CHAPTER FOURTEEN

The Long Shadow of Words

> If we had demanded of the Senate of Rome, of the Areopagus of Athens, or at the court of the kings of Persia: "Are you idolaters?," they would scarcely have understood the question.
>
> Voltaire, Philosophical Dictionary, "Idolatry"

I have used the term "polytheism" quite often in the preceding pages. But what does it exactly mean? A typical dictionary definition would show that polytheism is a combination of two Greek words—*polýs*, "many", and *theós*, "god"—and define it as "the belief in or worship of more than one god."[1] By using the word polytheism to indicate the religions of antiquity I have been, in truth, rather respectful. I have never spoken about them as "pagans" or "idolaters," terms that are still used today to indicate worshippers of ancient religions in all kinds of settings, even academic ones.[2] The terms polytheism, paganism, and idolatry have, without doubt, different connotations, but they do share something in common: none of them would have ever been used by a Roman or a Greek to indicate their own religions. All three terms, in fact, have their origins not within, but outside ancient religions. It would probably be even more accurate to say: *against* them.

In order to define oneself as a religious person who worshiped one's own gods, a Greek would have said he was *eusebés* ("respectful of the gods"), carrying out *tà tóis theóis nomizómena* ("the ceremonies owed to the gods by tradition") and practicing *tà hierá* ("sacred offerings or sacrifices"), cultivating *tà théia* ("divine things"), and so forth, but certainly he would not have defined himself as an "idolater" or even as a "polytheist." A Roman would have defined himself as *pius,* moved by the same "devotion" or "submission" that one feels towards one's father or family, and declared to *colere deos*, "worship the gods," to honor the *sacra* ("sacred things"), to observe the *ritus* ("the ritual habits"), the *caerimoniae* ("religious rites"), the *religio* ("ritual zeal" and "relationship with the divine"), but would certainly not have declared himself to be a "pagan."[3]

How did these terms come about, then, if neither the Greeks nor the Romans, I must stress, would have ever used them to define themselves as religious?

Let me begin with the term that I have used up to now, "polytheism." As just mentioned, this Greek word literally means "of many gods." But the first time this combination of "many" and "gods" was used was not by a Greek but by a Jew from Alexandria: Philo, the famous allegorist and commentator on the Bible. It was he who used expressions like *he polytheía,* "the multiplicity of the gods," *he polýtheos dóxa,* "the doctrine of many gods," *tò polýtheon,* "the multiplicity of the gods," and *ho polýtheos,* "he who worships many gods." His insistence on showing the others, the Gentiles, as being "people of many gods" is perfectly understandable from the perspective of someone who worshiped only one single God and could not imagine doing otherwise. For this kind of observer, the most representative feature of the Greek and Roman religions could be nothing other than the *multiplicity* of the gods that were worshiped. In addition, the contexts where Philo makes use of this kind of wording are always negative. Someone who professes *he polýtheos dóxa* turns the heavens into the most idiotic "ochlocracy" (what we would today call "populism") that you can find in bad governments, and this doctrine should never even be uttered in the presence of a man who seeks the truth; *tò polýtheon* is an evil thing that leads to atheism and is a vice on par with polyandry, a woman who has multiple husbands; and so forth.[4] As far as the Christian tradition goes, the definition of classical religion as being one marked by "many gods" resurfaced in particular with Pseudo-Justin, an author from the third century ("Orpheus, who of your *polytheótes,* as one might call it, is the greatest master") and in many other texts. In the Christian world as well, the negative connotations of the word are almost always made explicit; just consider the formulation of the compound noun *polytheomanía,* "the madness of worshipping many gods," as an example.[5]

Modern culture begins to use the term "polytheism" in 1580 with the writings of Jean Bodin, who does not use it to describe the religion of "pagans," as we might expect, but to describe Christian heresies like the Manichaeisms of Marcion and Basilides, who instead of believing in a single divine principle in the universe, argued for two, three, or even four (as a consequence, "Polytheisme est un droict Atheisme"). In England the word first appears in the work of Samuel Purchas in 1614, when he uses it to describe the worship of saints, images, and the communion wafer that "Papists and Jesuits" introduced in the New World, almost as if it were an "exchanged Polytheism."[6] At this point, it is necessary to reflect upon the term that in my opinion represents a kind of antonymic couple with polytheism: monotheism. This is another Greek word, composed of the parts *mónos,* "only one," and *theós*, "god." The person to coin the word this time, though, was not a Jew from Alexandria as one might expect, and not even a Greek observing the Jewish world with the eyes of a "polytheist," but an English theologian from the seventeenth century, Henry More. Before this expression entered into popular usage in modern society Jews and Christians had indeed defined the faith in a single god with words like "monarchy," and later on, "theism."[7] Even more surprisingly, we find that Henry More, the creator of the term, did not use it to define the religion of those who believe in a single god, in contrast to those who believe in many. On the contrary, he makes use of the term within the context of a critique against those "apologists of paganism" according to whom the ancients themselves were believers in a single—though nameless—god, as some statements by Plutarch would suggest. Against such apologists, More maintained that this presumed single god was in fact the world, the entire universe. This was the reason why "To make the World God is to make no God at all; and therefore this kind of Monotheisme of the Heathen is as rank Atheism as their Polytheisme was proven to be before."[8] In a later work, More would use "Monotheisme" to denigrate the Jews, who "destroy the worship of the Son of God under an ignorant pretense of Monotheisme."[9] More thus uses the term in order to (negatively) underline the fact that the Jews deny Jesus's divinity, and the reason for this lies in their obstinance in believing there is "only one" god.

As often happens when you examine the history of important terms used in intellectual debate, interesting and unexpected aspects come to light. These two terms, both so crucial to the modern debate on religion, loom over the horizon of modern culture in a rather paradoxical way. On the one side, polytheism, the term used to describe the religions of antiquity, was introduced in the modern period as a way to define certain Christian heresies, and even the cult of saints in Catholicism; on the other, monotheism, the term most commonly used to identify the three religions of a single god, was created in order to define a particular form of atheism found amongst the ancient "pagans," and even in a negative way to describe the belief in a single God as preached by the Jews.

Since I have just mentioned the pagans, I should ask where this term comes from as well. No Roman would have ever used it to identify himself as being devoted to the gods of his own city or family. In classical Latin, the adjective *paganus* means simply an inhabitant of a *pagus,* a "village," someone who lives in the countryside, in contrast to someone who lives in the city (*urbanus*). Among the Christian authors though, especially Augustine, *paganus* becomes the most common term to describe those who have remained faithful to traditional forms of worship, members of the *gentes* or the *nationes.* How did this strange change in meaning, from villager to 'pagan', take place? In truth, scholars have researched this aspect for a very long time, at least since the 1500s, when an initial explanation was briefly suggested in two lines by the jurist Andrea Alciati. Given that *paganus,* in legal jargon, was the opposite of *militaris* and that a Christian was often defined as *miles Christi,* "a soldier of Christ," the meaning of *paganus* as a "non-Christian" could have been born directly from this contrast: "the pagans are called such because they are not soldiers of Christ, just as in legal matters, those who are not soldiers, and who carry out their duties in towns and villages, are known as *pagani.*"[10] Approximately fifty years after Alciati, Cesare Baronio, in his *Martyrologium christianum,* suggested instead that Christians called people who didn't belong to the new religion *paganus* because traditional worship of the ancient gods had by then been relegated to the countryside, far from city centers.[11] Baronio had come to this conclusion after having discussed and dismissed other etymological hypotheses (like those put forward by Isidore of Seville and the Venerable Bede), and after carrying out a historical and philological analysis that still today commands admiration for its erudition and intelligence, even though some modern exegetes do not seem to have taken notice. However, one must admit that both Alciati's and Baronio's interpretations are not without their flaws.

Another possible explanation of this odd semantic slip from "villager" to "non-Christian" was put forward more recently by Christine Mohrmann. *Paganus*, aside from the meaning of "bourgeois," i.e., not a member of the army, was also used in the past to indicate the condition of someone *before* becoming a member of a certain group, *before* completing an action that would in some manner change his or her identity. This was why, for example, the names of gladiators before entering the ranks of their companions were known as "pagan names," which they would take on as new combat names. Similarly, someone who had no official status or public role, a "private citizen," could be called *paganus*. Ultimately, perhaps *paganus* comes from the need to designate those who were not (yet?) a part of the group, who were not "one of us," but just private citizens. It is hard to understand, in any event, why this connotation would have ended up being so successful.[12]

Now let me look at the terms "idolater" and "idolatry." These are compound Greek nouns, formed by the words *éidolon*, "image," and *latréuo*, "I adore, I worship." Thus the word *eidololátres* defined a person who "adores images," just as *eidololatría* defined the "worship of images."[13] Once again there is no need to point out how the Greeks themselves would never have used such a word to define their worship for a statue of one of their own gods. Like *polythéïa* and the other terms that gave life to our "polytheism," both *eidololátres* and *eidololatría* come from the Jewish side: not from Philo this time, but directly from the Greek translation of the Hebrew Bible, the Septuagint, carried out in Alexandria in the third century BCE. Where the original Hebrew text spoke of the prohibition to worship images of gods (as those who did not believe in a single god), the Greek translators chose the word *éidolon* to identify the object of such condemnation. Therefore the Septuagint translation marked the birth of those *éidola* that would be condemned in the Greek Christian tradition; of those *idola* against which the Latin apologists would combat; of those "idols" that would become the polemical target of later Christian culture, up to the contemporary use of the word even in unexpected contexts.[14] Yes, but what kind of image did the Alexandrian translators have in mind when they used the word *éidola* to describe the images worshiped by the Gentiles?

Actually, the word *éidolon* does not indicate any kind of real image, and even less a venerated statue. This word specifically defines an *inconstant* image, something vain, a trick, like those that appear to us in dreams, in the reflection of a mirror, in the fleeting shadow of the dead. Such a simulacrum pertains exclusively to the sense of sight (the word *éidolon* derives from the root *id-* "to see"), and as such is deceptive, ungraspable, just like the images of dreams or the shadows of the dead. Thus the use of the word *éidolon* to indicate the statues of the religions of "others" implicates from the very beginning an intrinsic condemnation: as *éidola,* the images worshiped by the Gentiles were automatically identified as vain and inconstant.[15]

The linguistic strategy chosen by the Alexandrian translators and followed by the Christian tradition—defining other people's religious images with a word implying automatically a judgment of falseness—was certainly adroit, but it is not unique. The same process unfolds in the use of the term "fetish" to identify the images or objects used by the so-called primitive religions. This word has its own interesting origins. Latin, indeed, uses a term, *facticius*, to designate a "fabricated" object, one created through an act of "making" (*facio*), in contrast to something "natural." In the Romance languages, this term gave birth to many other words—including the Portuguese *feitiço*—meaning something "artificial" in the sense that it had been created through magic.[16] The "making" that creates a "non-natural" object is thus identified with the "fabricating" of a witch or magician: an evil fabrication that upends nature through the use of occult powers. In the sixteenth century Portuguese explorers would use precisely the term *feitiço*—"magical, bewitched object"—to identify the religious objects used by the peoples of Guinea in West Africa.

Through this simple act of naming, the objects of religious worship belonging to a certain group of people would indeed maintain their link with the supernatural world—insofar as it acknowledged in them a certain effectiveness, albeit of a magical nature—but they were automatically downgraded to the ranks of objects created by witchcraft, and in this manner were denied any form of religious legitimacy. The Portuguese word, which became "fétiche" in French, enjoyed greater and greater popularity after Charles De Brosses made use of it (together with the nouns "fétichisme" and "fétichiste") to identify the most primitive stage of human religious history, one including the worship of objects or animals.[17] This is not the place to carry out a fuller examination of the history of a word that has also had an incredibly strong influence within anthropological and historical-religious fields (not to mention others: just consider Marx's "commodity fetishism" or the "fetishism" of paraphilia in Freudian psychoanalysis).[18] What interests me here is to point out how using the words *éidolon* (= vain and inconstant image) for the statues of Gentile or pagan religion, or *feitiço* (= a product of witchcraft) for an object or image venerated by African peoples, and by so-called primitives in general, both utilize the same strategy of tacitly demeaning other peoples' religions by linguistic means.

What conclusion can be drawn from what I have described so far? Words truly cast a long shadow, and this shadow is capable of hiding, altering, and deforming the reality of the objects that they designate. Let me do a quick summary. As shown, "polytheism," "paganism," and "idolatry" are all words that were created within the culture of a single god. Therefore, using them to speak about the religion of the Greeks and Romans means, at the very best, to speak about them from a Jewish or Christian perspective; and at the worst, to give a demeaning image of the ancient religions. This latter aspect is particularly clear with "idolatry" (the parallel with "fetish" is rather eloquent), but remains valid for "paganism" as well. If at least at the beginning, the adjective *paganus*—to designate a non-Christian—did not seem to have particularly offensive connotations, the way it has been used subsequently in our cultural history has nonetheless given the term pagan—and its related terms in various modern languages—a negative aura. It is hard to ignore its use in the title of one of the most significant works by such an important author as Augustine: *On the City of God Against the Pagans.* The first lines of his preface make reference to "the worshipers of false gods, or pagans, as we commonly call them."[19] To define the religion of the Greeks and Romans as "paganism" inevitably evokes the ghost of idolatry, with all the trappings of superstition, falsehood, and immoral behavior that Christianity has saddled it with.[20] Just think of the figurative use still made today of "pagan gods" or "idols" when speaking about the moral depravations afflicting the world, as when someone condemns the "god of money" or the "goddess of bribes" or tries to convince people to spurn the "idols" of power or richness. Even if we agree that bribes and power games are blameworthy, we cannot help but notice how similar images perpetuate a distorted and degrading vision of ancient religion.[21] In a different context, the use of phrases like "pagan literature," "pagan historiography," or "pagan classics," is equally unjustifiable when talking about the cultural products of the third, fourth, or fifth centuries CE, almost as if the identifying characteristic of these artifacts were simply the fact of *not* being inspired by Christianity.[22]

As for the term polytheism—currently the most commonly used by academics and generally considered the most appropriate—it does not seem to be perceived as being particularly disparaging toward ancient religions. All the same, this term itself is not free from its shadows. When we represent the religions of the Greeks and of the Romans as polytheistic, we nonetheless continue to make use of a vocabulary provided from those who worship a single and exclusive god, and we end up, more or less consciously, sustaining the idea that the most important element of ancient religious systems is "the many gods," thus partaking in the same vision of an ancient Jewish or a Christian apologist. As mentioned, though, these systems have many other qualities, many of which I have tried to put front and center in this book. The gods who were worshiped were not only "many," they were also interpretable, translatable, borrowable, exchangeable, able to be combined in different forms, all according to a general principle of flexibility and pliancy. The latter feature is an integral part of the ancient religions, and in my opinion, when we no longer examine these religions through the lens of a single god, it is equally if not more relevant than the fact that their gods were "many."[23] The plurality of gods did not constitute the *essence* of polytheistic religions as the name would make us believe, but merely the necessary condition for bringing forth their most important virtue: the capacity to think in a plural fashion about the world around them and, at the same time, to provide equally plural methods for interpreting and intervening in this world.[24]

CHAPTER FIFTEEN

The Twilight of Writing, the Sunset of Scripture

The arguments I have laid forth so far show (at least I hope they do) that the appropriation of certain polytheistic ways of thinking can offer a "cash-value" for societies in which monotheistic religions are currently active—like our own—and where they have historically marked our culture and thought. Tools such as translatability, borrowing, and reciprocal *interpretatio* of the divine would reduce the extent of conflict between different monotheistic religions and between their internal subdivisions. Moreover, curiosity toward the gods of others and the desire to get to know them, even to naturalize them, would provide new lifeblood to what we call "interfaith dialogue." Similarly, the practice of *interpretatio,* alongside the Roman conception according to which foreign gods deserved to be granted "citizenship," would offer a different vision of religious tolerance, a concept that still contains certain equivocations since its original conception. But it is pointless now to repeat what I have already said. Rather, let me formulate the last question I would like to try to answer: would the great monotheistic religions be capable of doing what we hope?

Even if we assume it to be possible, it is obvious that there would nonetheless be numerous, arduous obstacles in the way. First of all, they would have to take into account the will of their hierarchies, who most likely would have very little interest in seeing their respective religions adhere to some form of a system of free exchange. Second, we cannot forget how millennia of history have transformed the various religions we are referring to into genuine "hereditary conglomerates," to borrow the phrase coined by Gilbert Murray and Eric R. Dodds.[1] Each of them has sedimented into specific visions of the world, ethnic characteristics, food traditions, languages, ceremonies, sexual practices, and so on, all of which are ready to intervene like an armored vehicle to clear the road of barricades like *interpretatio* and the borrowing of a god, practices that tend toward exchange and intermixing. As we have shown, placing the relationship between different religions onto the plane of "true" versus "false," as happens in monotheism, favors forms of ethnocentrism and cultural closure.[2] But aside from these cultural incompatibilities—the only ones, by the way, invoked when the subject of the difficulty of religion communication comes up—the obstacles in our hypothetical path are specifically *structural* incompatibilities, as I would define them. The latter create the basis for cultural incompatibilities, and they regulate their working principles as well.

First off, the unique and exclusive concept of the divine that represents the backbone of monotheism: this vision of the divine is always the largest stumbling block to activating polytheistic potential within a monotheistic setting. The commandment "I am the Lord your God [...] you shall have no other gods before me" is common to Jews and Christians, while Islam asks its faithful to affirm that "Allah bears witness that there is no god but He."[3] Even within Catholicism the principle of uniqueness, truth, authenticity, and absolute sovereignty of God is clearly indicated. It would be natural, though, to think that in reality, a gap exists between the strictness of certain "official" stances and the common sense of everyday people, a sort of assumption that we can take the "Mosaic exclusion" less literally than what it would demand. If you are not an American televangelist, you don't always have a copy of the Bible at hand nor do you always have Biblical verses at the tip of your tongue. I do not at all exclude the possibility of a "fluid" perception of the Mosaic distinction; the problem is that even here, assimilating polytheistic ways of thinking by monotheistic religions would nevertheless run into a second structural obstacle: *scripture.* In other words, those absolutist declarations about the uniqueness of God are all written down in each of the "books" forming the basis of the three monotheistic religions, and therefore any divergent position from what is recorded therein would be contradicted, sooner or later. We are well aware of the social force traditionally exerted by scripture, just like the power inherently possessed by the letters of the alphabet, capable of preserving and transmitting information *ad infinitum.* As Carlo Severi writes, "the relationship established between a primary text and its source (mythical or real) absolutely resides at the origin of the Western idea of authority."[4] "What is written" is also "what matters."

Countless examples show how this binding characteristic of *texts* continues to actively influence contemporary experience within monotheistic cultures. I will mention only one example that caused a certain sensation in France a few years ago. In 2003, a famous Muslim intellectual, Tariq Ramadan, debated on national television with Nicolas Sarkozy, when he was Minister of the Interior. Sarkozy pointedly asked Ramadan whether he condemned the stoning of adulterers, and the answer he received was the following. Personally, I am against capital punishment, Ramadan said, not only in Muslim nations but also in the US. But if you want to be listened to in Muslim nations when you speak about religious issues, it is not enough to just state that capital punishment must end. I think it must end. But this issue needs to be debated within its religious context. *There are texts involved.*[5]

Let me pause to look more closely at these "texts," the "scriptures" at the base of monotheistic religions. They are commonly called "sacred," and when people talk about polytheism, they are always quick to mention how the ancient religions did not have anything comparable. This is an extremely important observation, one that reminds us how in antiquity, religious rules were part of the norms and customs of a city—just like laws or wedding statutes—and not a separate corpus sectioned off in a book considered sacred.[6] Perhaps, though, when talking about the "religions of the book," as they are known, the mere use of the adjective "sacred" is not enough. It would seem in fact preferable to highlight the fact that this book, more than simply sacred, is a book *inspired* and *written* directly *by God.* Examining this theme allows me to underline one last but fundamental difference between monotheistic and polytheistic ways of thinking, and to understand more precisely what the absence of "sacred" books means for ancient religions.

In a chapter from the *Apologeticus,* written in Carthage towards the end of the 2nd century, Tertullian wrote:

> But that we might more fully and more seriously approach to [God] as well as to his arrangements and purposes, he added the tool of writing (*instrumentum litteraturae*), in case anyone should wish to inquire about God, and having inquired to find him, and having found him to believe on him, and having believed to serve him. For from the beginning he hath sent into the world men overflowing

> with the divine spirit, and worthy by their justice and innocence to know God and to make him known, in order that they might preach him as the only god who founded the universe, and formed man from the soil,—for this is the true Prometheus.... Those whom we have called preachers (*praedicatores*) are named prophets from their office of foretelling (*praefari*). Their words and likewise their wonderful deeds, which they performed to produce belief in the Godhead, remain in the storehouses of literature (*in thesaurus litterarum*), nor are these now hidden.[7]

The Christian God, and before him the God of the Jews, had spoken *in order to be recorded:* he made use of writing (*litteratura*), of the letters of the alphabet, so that the words and the works of the prophets inspired by him would be written down and preserved. In this manner, men received a significantly more powerful tool, we suppose, than dreams or visions in their quest to approach God. But to say that God, in order to make himself manifest, had simply made use of the "tool" of *litteratura* is not enough. The *instrumentum* he chose to use is something indeed much more complex. What this word suggests is not only the tool used for communication, or a *corpus* of texts capable of "instructing," of making other people aware: it is *proof.* In the language of Roman jurists, in fact, *instrumentum* meant also the entire set of materials—witness statements, documents, even people themselves—that could be used to "build" a case.[8] The *litteratura* used by God was thus not merely a tool for communication or doctrine, but a method within a universal legal case that should lead to the most supreme of conclusions: "that He is the only God, that everything was created by Him, that He gave form to man from the earth." Herein lies Tertullian's point of view about the book of the Christians: *litteratura*, much more than just a straightforward accumulation of letters from the alphabet, made a record of words and facts in order to enrich knowledge. It was a demonstration. The fact then that by the word *instrumentum* one could specifically indicate sacred scripture (or its two parts: *instrumentum vetus, instrumentum novum*)[9] made it even clearer how this book bore no resemblance to other books of antiquity—works by historians, philosophers, or poets—but was much more. Or, to put it better, it was something profoundly different from a simple book.

A God who leaves a written record represents a great cultural shift. In the classical world such a phenomenon was practically unheard of: the gods had never manifested or expressed themselves through a book. In Greece and in Rome the relationship between the divine and the human word seems somehow *reversed* compared to what we are used to thinking about the Jewish or the Christian cultures. As we have seen, according to Tertullian, *litteratura* is directly linked to God; he manifests existence, virtue, and qualities through the *thesauri litterarum*—the book of which God is the direct author. In the Christian world (as would also be the case later on in the Islamic world), God has become the "author" of the book about himself, and he has taken textual responsibility for it. He therefore also *owns* it entirely. This feature will powerfully influence even the Western conception of translation, that as a consequence of this change of perspective emphasizes a meticulous attention to being faithful to the original text.[10]

On the other hand, in Greece and Rome the authorship of discourses about the gods was never assumed by the deities themselves, but by *men:* the gods did not speak of themselves, it was men who spoke of them, and thus it is equally men who were the authors and owners of the words placed in the gods' mouths. Herodotus demonstrates this quite clearly in a rather famous passage:

> But whence each of the gods came to be, or whether all had always been, and how they appeared in form, they did not know until yesterday or the day before, so to speak; for I suppose Hesiod and Homer flourished not more than four hundred years earlier than I; and these are the ones who taught the Greeks the descent of the gods, and gave the gods their names, and determined their spheres and functions, and described their outward forms.[11]

It is poets who introduced us to the gods, who described the forms in which they took shape, their spheres of influence, the offerings that were owed to them, and so forth. Revealingly, for the Greeks, it is men who own the words about the divine that God claims for himself in the Jewish and Christian tradition. Revelation is not divine, but human, and moreover, fairly recent. In a world in which the gods are not concerned about speaking in order to be recorded, the task of teaching the world about the epithets, glories, and abilities of the gods belongs to poets, who have not "been preaching" since the beginning of time—*a primordio,* as Tertullian says about the prophets of Israel—, but for no more than four hundred years before Herodotus. It's no surprise if Josephus, in a passage already quoted, cannot but consider this attitude a mistake on the part of the Greeks, who,

> as if it were a thing of very little consequence, gave leave both to the poets to introduce what gods they pleased, and those subject to all sorts of passions, and to the orators to procure political decrees from the people for the admission of such foreign gods as they thought proper. The painters also, and statuaries of Greece, had herein great power, as each of them could contrive a shape [proper for a god].[12]

Even the Romans had a substantially similar attitude toward the affairs of the gods, with a very relevant difference: in a culture where the *civitas* was decisively more important than poets, the credit given by Herodotus to Homer and Hesiod was rather bestowed on public institutions. I have already cited the words of Augustine about Varro:

> He wrote first concerning human things, but afterwards concerning divine things, because the states (*civitates*) existed first, and afterward these things were instituted by them.[13]

It is the same as before: "discourses" about the gods, just as the rites performed for them, have people as their authors, not the gods themselves.

I can thus confidently state that the primary obstacle to the adoption of polytheistic ways of thinking by monotheisms, perhaps even more so than the Mosaic exclusivity, is the fact that the monotheistic religion was *written* in a book whose *author* is *God*. As the *Catechism of the Catholic Church* still reads today, "God is the *author* of Sacred Scripture."[14] In a situation such as this, scripture—understood as the recording of information through the use of the letters of the alphabet—reveals the full strength of its power, but also its tendency to create limits. Turning God into the author of the "book" about himself gives this text an authority and power unheard of. Certainly neither the *Theogony* of Hesiod nor the *Antiquities of Human and Divine Things* of Varro—no matter how influential they were—could ever have dreamed of such a thing. At the same time, bestowing divine nature on "what is written" inhibits the possibility of formulating new and different representations of God, except (as in fact has happened) through a lengthy labor of *internal* exegesis of the book itself: a process undertaken in different forms both in Christianity and Islam over the centuries. This process remains, however, characterized by exclusivity, a fundamental datum of monotheism, and thus undertakes a search for truth not *outside* the book of God but *within* it, a truth that in each circumstance insists upon being *deeper within* the book than previous formulations had been.

On the other hand, considering that in polytheistic cultures the word about the divine belongs to men and not to the gods, the possibility always exists for adjusting, expanding, or even rewriting the discourse of gods. And this is absolutely the structural core that opens polytheism to the set of possibilities I have described in the previous chapters, from "translation" of foreign gods to the opportunity to "interpret one into another," and so on. In order for the great monotheistic religions to internalize some of these specifically polytheistic ways of thinking, they would need, in some way, to loosen the knot that sits at the heart of their structure, gripping it on one side with the natural *authority* possessed by *scripture,* and on the other with the added strength that the *author* of this scripture is God himself.

Considering all I have already said, it nevertheless becomes interesting to observe how the times in which we are living, and even more so the ones we have in front of us, contain a flurry of signs that writing, as a means of communication, is losing importance. Book and newspaper sales are dropping every day, meagerly compensated for by ebooks and online journals, while communication of a personal, direct manner, made available by smartphones, ipads, and similar devices, is having its moment of glory. The human voice and the presence of interlocutors have found an extremely powerful ally in digital technology, one that no longer forces to rely solely upon the letters of the alphabet to transmit what we need to learn from or make known to others, and which allows us to use our natural communicative resources (eyes, ears, tongue, hand gestures, etc.) without the restriction of being physically present in a given place. Moreover, the archival recording of information, which for millennia has been dominated exclusively by the alphabet, is becoming more and more dependent upon the images, audio recordings, and video clips that are replacing the written document. It is not accidental then that today, the most frequent use of the noun "book" is within the word "facebook," a "book of faces," not of the alphabet, as a clear indication of what is meant today by the word "book": something "written" by a personal and direct dialogue with the visible circle of one's own acquaintances.

We are witnessing the twilight not of the book, as people often claim, but of *writing*—of *scriptura, litteratura*—in general, replaced by minimal fragments of itself, in the form of texts or tweets, or even more directly through voices, images, virtual productions, and so on. The sun is not setting on the book, but on the *text,* understood as a broad architecture of enunciations with which a reader undertakes a communicative act able to last over time, often over long periods of time: the time required for a mute voice of an author to be heard within a reader's mind and memory. Behind today's vanishing of books from shelves and the growing reduction in their sizes—behind the anxious search for an instant bestseller and the success of books/non-books produced by authors whose only merit is media visibility—resides the decline of syntax in favor of bytes, the replacement of sentences by a "person" or by his or her image. It is pointless to add that if this is truly the direction in which our society is headed, as it seems, I don't know how much there is to be happy about. In the meantime, I can only hope that the final gloaming will last long enough to allow us to transport all or part of those treasures of memory and culture preserved for us by writing throughout the millennia into this new dimension. I have to hope, let me be frank, that the sun doesn't set too quickly.

These days, though, are not only bringing us into the twilight of writing, but perhaps even more remarkably, into the end of the *author*. The universe of the media, in particular digital media, seems ever more dominated by anonymity, by pseudonyms, by identity theft: who really knows anymore who is at the origin of what, in this unstoppable whirlpool of data flow that we all find ourselves swimming in? "The idea of an author is foreign to the web," we often hear repeated on this score, and the rule of *copyleft* (an elegant and "liberal" play on words) expands often into the direction of genuine *copytheft*. The gradual disappearance of "authorship" as a category presents a problem that, as is well known, keeps scholars of intellectual rights just as busy as copyright holders trying to rein in products that circulate and bounce about web platforms ever more freely. This gradual sunset of the author does not present solely a legal or financial problem, but also, and even more relevantly, a moral question. What happens when, alongside the concept of authorship, we concomitantly lose the intrinsic implications of the relationship between the author and his work: the public, collective *responsibility* for the claims the author makes or the stands the author takes?[15]

From this vantage point—the twilight of writing and of the author—let me try to return to the theme of this final chapter: the possibility for the great monotheistic religions to assimilate polytheistic ways of thinking, and the obstacles inevitably standing in the way of this process. In my opinion these obstacles are first and foremost the "written" words in the Book of monotheisms and especially in their author, who is considered to be God himself. The general cultural transformation under our eyes—which includes in equal parts writing, authorship, and the responsibility for the sentences one writes—elicits a scenario that we had not expected, unforeseeable, even inconceivable just a few years ago. In other words, it opens up the possibility that even in the field of religion, the importance of "what is written" may weaken alongside the broader cultural tendency gradually eroding the privileges traditionally bestowed upon the alphabet. In a world in which (even in the universities) the history textbook seems to be more and more enriched, and sometimes even substituted, by historical movies, and the great documents of literature are ever more frequently reworked into television series, animation, or some virtual mix, it would not be strange to think that even "what is written" in the Book of religions will become more and more replaced by "what can been seen" in its visual and/or virtual reworkings. On the other hand, it is equally possible that the other tendency active in contemporary society, the twilight of the concept of authorship, could eventually touch even the figure of the divine Author, thereby inevitably weakening his position as the bedrock of absolute responsibility for "what is written." The enormous communicative transformation we are living may end up standing in conflict with a monotheistic religious tradition that has given to the two paradigms of Scripture and Author a determining, central, and absolute role. In such a context, where even the Book and its divine Author would acquire a more opaque, indefinite quality, it would therefore become less difficult for new religious models to slip through the cracks of a *writing/scripture* increasingly diluted in images and sounds.

APPENDIX A

RELIGIOUS TOLERANCE AND INTOLERANCE IN THE ANCIENT WORLD

Can we apply the idea of religious tolerance/intolerance—so familiar to modern culture—to the classical world? This is a well-debated question among historians of ancient religion, and of Christianity in particular, and too complex to approach in a brief appendix. But I can attempt to narrow the question down to the aspect that most interests me: the comparison between polytheistic and monotheistic ways of thinking.

Let me begin then with "tolerance." Clearly it would be out of place to use this concept in order to define the actions of classical societies, and not only because the idea itself was unknown in the ancient world, having been created at the beginning of the fifth century in a Christian cultural context. The most important aspect is that polytheistic societies, by definition, allow for a plurality of gods, and to differing extents recognize or even assimilate the gods of others. Therefore, when describing their openness in terms of religious matters, we cannot speak merely of "tolerance," if by this term we mean the attitude of someone who refrains from repressing religious forms of which they nonetheless disapprove. This would be an insufficient label at best, and at worst a misleading one, unless we make use of it in the formula suggested by Peter Garnsey: "toleration by default."[1] But even this would not change the terms of the question.

The problem represented by applying the term "religious intolerance" to the ancient world is more complicated. The expression is often used to explain Roman historical facts such as the repression of the *Bacchanalia* and, later on, the anti-Christian persecutions (to which we can add the accusations and attacks made against the worship of Serapis, Isis, or Bellona over the years). Persecutions similar to those carried out in monotheistic lands can be identified, but the motivations behind them are quite different. The repression of the *Bacchanalia*, for example, was not set off because the god himself (Bacchus) was considered a false, lying, or demonic divinity, and much less because his followers refused to venerate a single true god, but because of the immoral nature of the *ceremonies* that were dedicated to this god. These ceremonies, according to the political authorities, distracted citizens from their religious duties toward the gods of the city, thereby endangering the *pax deorum.* The entire Roman population was considered at risk when certain impious acts were carried out by a group or even a single person.

Moreover, ceremonies of this sort threatened the very existence of the *res publica,* forming groups that followed different laws from those of the state and giving rise to conspiratorial plots. As the Maecenas of Cassius Dio suggested to Augustus, whoever rules must keep an eye on "foreign practices, from which spring up conspiracies, factions, and cabals."[2] This was the spirit by which Roman state authority monitored what was acceptable or desirable for its citizens in terms of religious practices (even if in Rome there was never an official list of authorized religions). In Rome, the cases of religious repression were first and foremost motivated by *political* reasons and not religious ones in the modern sense of the word because politics—conceived as one with the laws and customs of the city—was the religion of the Romans.

As for the complex phenomenon of anti-Christian persecution, it is well-known that in this case what pulled the trigger of "intolerance" (if we really must use this term) was both the state's fear in dealing with a dangerous group like the Bacchics, and its impossibility of accepting the Christian refusal to make sacrifices to the gods of the city. This is proof of how in the Roman mindset, the dividing line between civic and religious duties is quite difficult to identify. According to Arnobius's testimony, this was the most common accusation made against the Christians: "If you are in earnest about religion, why do you not serve and worship the other gods with us, or share your sacred rites with your fellows, and put the ceremonies of the different religions on an equality?"[3] The stakes here lie in the turning away from things that are *commune,* the rejection of sharing, of *miscere,* of *coniungere* and thereby neglecting the *sacra* that belong to the Roman state and are identified with the very life of the City. From this perspective, an interesting parallel, maybe more illuminating than others, comes to us from the 1900s. After the cult of the Emperor was developed in modern Japan, local Christians found themselves in a position analogous to their earliest brethren: they were in fact accused of not showing loyalty to the nation, and were forced to choose between their God and the Emperor.[4]

Going back to the repression of the *Bacchanalia,* let me look closely at the text of the *Senatusconsultum* from 186 BCE.[5] Reading through the lens of modern "intolerance," one cannot help but be surprised. At the same time the *Bacchanalia* was being suppressed, there was a discussion going on about what to do in the event that someone believed it nonetheless necessary to celebrate the rituals of Bacchus, because not doing so could constitute an act of "impiety" (*piaculum*). In such a situation, the celebration would be allowed, but only after following a procedure with strict requirements: the participation of the city praetor, a ruling by the Senate (made in the presence of at least one hundred senators), the limitation to no more than five participants, a ban on using public funds, and the final requirement that the officiant be either a *magister sacrorum* or a priest. As is clear, what was called into question was not the god himself, since in some cases what was considered "impious" was *not* to worship him, but the way in which he was worshiped, which had to be strictly regulated. What is more, the decree calls for the destruction of the places in which the *Bacchanalia* were celebrated, first in Rome and then throughout Italy, but makes an exception "for those places where there were ancient altars or consecrated statues," meaning the religious symbols related to Bacchus *pre-dating* the new wave of rituals deemed dangerous. The decision was not to destroy *tout court* the statues and altars of another god, condemned simply by default (as would have happened applying the commandments of Exodus), but only those where the rituals judged unacceptable and dangerous were performed. After all, the few extant examples we have of religious satire from antiquity (regarding the goddess Sira or the cult of Cybele) share the same attitude: the target is not the goddess, but the ways in which her followers worship her. In this regard, we find the satirical description of the miller's wife in Apuleius quite interesting. She is most probably a Christian, attacked because "she detested and scorned the heavenly powers, and in place of established (*certa*) religion presumed to worship a false and sacrilegious deity she called the 'only god', inventing fantastic rites to make fun of everyone."[6] As can be seen, the criticism is focused on the fact that the woman, in proclaiming her faith in an only god, detested and scorned the gods of the *certa* religion: the gods of the city. The logic is the same as the one behind the repression of the *Bacchanalia*.[7]

As seen above, the accusations thrown at the Christians, according to Arnobius, could basically be boiled down to a single form: the Christians acted *exclusively*, because they excluded the gods of the city from their prayers and worship. This led to an inevitable reaction by the authorities. From this perspective, what strikes us most is the fact that, well over seven hundred years earlier, a similar phenomenon had occurred in Rome, brought about by equally similar causes. According to a tale by Livy, in 430 BCE, following a period of great drought and the arrival of terrible diseases, Rome was overwhelmed by a flood of superstitions (*multiplex religio*) mostly of foreign origin. The leading citizens of the city were forced to recognize that

> in every street and chapel (*omnibus ... sacellis*) outlandish and unfamiliar sacrifices were being offered up to appease Heaven's anger. [12] The aediles were then commissioned to see to it that none but Roman gods (*nisi Romani di*) should be worshipped, nor in any but the ancestral way.[8]

This situation did not simply imply banning *religious practices* of foreign origin, without however denying the legitimacy of the gods being worshipped, as had happened on the contrary with Bacchus and the Bacchanalia. In 420 BCE, the aediles specifically prohibited the worship of foreign gods, ruling that only Roman gods could be venerated (and only by using local rituals).

Let me look more closely, though, at the way Livy describes the situation that had arisen in Rome, in particular this adjective *omnibus,* which is accompanied by the word *sacellis.* The notables had realized that all of the sacred spaces had been occupied by foreign gods, in essence eliminating Roman gods from worship. This was not a case of *also* worshiping gods from other places, a situation that would have been considered more or less normal, especially during a period of upheaval, but of *only* worshiping foreign gods, elbowing the Roman gods out of sacred places. We find ourselves once again in front of a phenomenon of *exclusion* to the detriment of the gods of the city, as would happen centuries later with Christianity, which hoped to remove traditional gods from the practice of worship in order to leave space for a foreign god (this time, though, only one, the *only* one). If Roman culture is capable of welcoming foreign gods within itself—and we have seen that this happened frequently—this does not mean that it can accept that its own gods be totally *substituted* by others that come from elsewhere. The fact that the same reaction took place at a distance of so many centuries—under a similar context and for analogous reasons—demonstrates that this kind of reaction comes from the deepest levels of Roman culture: it is a question of structure, not of chance.

Still related to the theme of ancient "religious intolerance," a further problem arises with regards to what the Christians, after a long period of being persecuted, would themselves do to the pagans, Jews, or heretics from the fourth century onward. Along these lines, historians of Christianity continue to ask questions about the following contradiction: if on one hand Christianity is a religion that professes love for your neighbor, and even for your enemy, on the other, it persecuted those who refused to accept the message of Christ or who practiced an undesirable variation of it. As has been written, Christians "changed from lambs to lions."[9] The explanations given by academics about this Christian intolerance are many: they suggest reasons based on theology or ideology (faith in a single true god), on history (the assumption of political power by Christians after Constantine), on sociology (the inner dynamics of any community trying to decisively affirm its own identity), or on a combination of these. In some cases, the interpretation is so "sophisticated" as to identify the seeds of aggression within the very doctrine of love: "the source of Christian intolerance should not be looked for in the idea of a single god, but in the implicit totalitarianism of an injunction to love that excludes no one within the entire human population."[10]

Whatever the reason, the contradiction remains, and it seems even starker when we consider that the second-century Christian authors speak to us with voices inclined toward meekness, supporting religious conversion as an interior choice not brought on by force, which would not suit God. Thus the Christian thinkers, before the era of their own intolerance, had had time to express ideas much more in line with the "injunction to love" compared to those that would follow. In the works by Tertullian we find clear reference to the value of religious freedom, to such a degree that some observers think he had developed a new principle prophetically presaging "the modern solutions of European liberalism."[11] As a matter of fact we owe the expression *libertas religionis* specifically to Tertullian, who seems to have coined it, not to mention phrases such as: "Neither indeed is it the business of religion to compel religion, which ought to be taken up willingly."[12] To fully appreciate this statement by Tertullian, however, we should not forget the historical context: he was acting and writing in a period when Christianity was still in a position of weakness, while the phenomena of intolerance we are considering would only come out after Christianity had reversed its fortunes and become dominant. From the point of view I am interested in, though, the observation that I must make is another. Tertullian's statement ("Neither indeed is it the business of religion to compel religion, which ought to be taken up willingly") is indeed preceded by the following sentences: "We worship *the One God,* whom, by nature, you all know.... *Others* also there are whom you believe to be gods, and whom we know to be *demons.*" In other words, at the very moment of extolling religious freedom, the unique truth of the Christian God is reaffirmed at the expense of the pagan gods. The Mosaic exclusion remains no matter what.[13]

APPENDIX B

THE UPS AND DOWNS OF *PAGANUS*

Cesare Baronio developed his interpretation of the term *paganus* with brilliant erudition, as well as with great modesty, stating he would readily change his opinion whenever someone else put forward a better solution. As it turned out, though, his explanation became the most widely accepted by modern scholars: *paganus* to indicate "non-Christians" would descend from the fact that the devotees of the ancient gods had become synonymous with the people who lived in the countryside. It is a shame, however, that Baronio's interpretation is often cited with a misunderstanding of the author's intent, or undercutting the richness of his arguments, or even forgetting that he came up with the idea in the first place. For example, Christine Mohrmann, in the best essay on this question, repeats some of Baronio's philological arguments without acknowledging their paternity. David Cameron remarkably attributes to Baronio the idea that the pagans were known as "country folks" because Christians "dismissed non-believers contemptuously as country bumpkins," as "coarse" and "uncouth" people. Baronio in no way says this; his is a historical, not a moral, interpretation: "quod legibus imperatorum clausis idolorum delubris.... Gentiles sua ipsorum superstitione exclusi, pagos adirent, illicque suos deos colerent, ac clandestina sacra peragerent." Baronio's pagans are not provincial farmers who were obtuse because they were still attached to the worship of gods, but devotees of an ancient religion who had abandoned the cities to take refuge in countryside villages after years of persecution and imperial laws. As for Polymnia Athanassiadi and Michael Frede, although they reprise Baronio's thesis, not only do they not quote it, but they even give *paganus,* in classical Latin, the meaning of "unlearned": a mistake that a full reading of Baronio would certainly have helped them to avoid. It is equally surprising to see two specialists of late antiquity attributing the first sentence of the *Praefatio* of *De civitate dei* by Augustine—a rather famous sentence—to *De corona militis* by Tertullian (?).[1]

With regards to the relative difficulties of the two prevailing explanations, those by Alciati and Baronio, Cameron has observed about Alciati's interpretation (where *paganus* is a contrast for *miles Christi*) that the identification of Christians by the name *miles Christi* is typical of Tertullian, but that the latter never uses *paganus* in the sense of "non-Christian." On the contrary, when *paganus* comes to be used in this sense later on, between the fourth and fifth centuries, the definition of a Christian as *miles Christi* had already long disappeared. Moreover, while the latter belongs to a high, literary register, the adjective *paganus* in the sense of non-Christian was used in the most common and widely spoken form of the language (*vulgo*). Between the two expressions lies not only a large chronological gap, but an equally wide linguistic one.[2]

As for Baronio's interpretation (that the *paganus,* as followers of the ancient gods, lived in the countryside), Mohrmann has identified a possible temporal discrepancy. In fact, *pagani* as "non-Christian" comes into being precisely during the period in which there is a decisively "urban" reaction against Christianity, led by the nobility and the schools. It seems surprising, therefore, that the origins of calling non-Christians "people who live in the countryside" would be at exactly the same moment when an attachment to traditional religion was appearing with particular strength in the cities.[3] It would have been more likely, it seems, to expect the opposite.

NOTES

INTRODUCTION

1. See chapter 14.

2. "Ancient religions are neither less spiritually rich nor less complex and intellectually organized than those today" (Vernant, *Mito e religione in Grecia antica,* 8, our translation). On the idea of how "religiosity," understood as the expression of an emotion or of an interior adherence to the divine, has been denied in particular to Roman religion see Scheid, *Les dieux, l'État et l'individu,* 41–49, 82–89, 175–93.

3. Leopardi, *Zibaldone,* II:2157, our translation.

4. Gladigow, "Polytheism," 1466–71.

5. Heine, "The Gods in Exile," 178.

6. Pater, *Imaginary Portraits.*

7. See Calasso, *Literature and the Gods.*

8. For the paragraphs that follow I found invaluable information in Bittarello, "Western Suspicion of Polytheism"; Calasso, *Literature and the Gods;* not to mention Detienne, "Du polythéisme en général."

9. For the letters between Goethe and Max Jacobi see Gladigow, "Polytheism." Quotation is from Hegel, "The Oldest Systematic Program of German Idealism."

10. Nietzsche, *The Gay Science,* 143, 191–92. See Funkenstein, "The Polytheism of William James," on the differences between Nietzsche and James in their respective appeals to polytheism. See also Heinrichs, "Full of Gods;" Gladigow, "Polytheism."

11. Jung, "European Commentary," 111–12.

12. Hillman, "On the Necessity of Abnormal Psychology", 93–94. In particular, Jungian psychology values polytheism for the aspect of pluralism that it is capable of giving to the psyche, which is to say for its use as a tool that can modulate the repressive "monism" of the ego, of reason, of consciousness, of the control center: see Drob, "The Depth of the Soul," 69, cited in Bittarello, "Western Suspicion of Polytheism," 79. On the work of D. L. Miller, *The New Polytheism: Rebirth of the Gods and Goddesses,* which was itself quite influential in its day (1974), and is equally focused on the psychic dimension of polytheism, see also Gladigow, "Polytheism." On the psychological use of polytheism, we should not forget the acute (even cutting) observations made by Detienne in "Du polythéisme en général."

13. Mallarmé, our translation.

14. Pound, *Guide to Kulchur,* epigraph.

15. Pound, *Guide to Kulchur,* 299, emphasis ours.

16. Pessoa, *Il ritorno degli dèi [The Return of the Gods*], our translation.

17. Marquard, "In Praise of Polytheism."

18. Tabucchi, "Elogio della letteratura," our translation.

19. Funkenstein, "The Polytheism of William James."

20. Cotkin, "William James and the Cash-Value Metaphor," 40.

21. For more on the "minuscule gods" (*dei minuti*) of the Romans, see Perfigli, *Indigitamenta,* and M. Bettini, "Ad negotia humana compositi. *L'agency humaine des dieux antiques*"; on the various spheres of influence of Mars, see Dumézil, *Archaic Roman Religion.*

22. By "ways of thinking" we mean those thought configurations that, within any given culture, are put into action at the moment of considering, organizing, and making use of a determined behavior, recommending certain mental processes and denying others.

23. De Tocqueville, our translation.

24. On neo-pagan movements see, for example, Faber and Schlesier, *Die Restauration der Götter,* and in particular, for a scholar whose

work focuses specifically on these phenomena, the conclusion in Bittarello, "Western Suspicion of Polytheism,".

CHAPTER ONE

1. *Il Giornale*, December 21, 2008. Other controversies arose during the 2013 festivities following the proposal, once again in schools, to abolish certain Christmas songs: *la Repubblica* (Firenze), December 12, 2013. It is reasonable to assume that the phenomenon is destined to repeat itself in the future.

2. "I Musulmani e le festività cristiane del Natale," December 7, 2010, http://domenicobuffarini.blogspot.it/2010/12; *Corriere della Sera*, December 23, 2004.

3. On the legal issues raised by the presence of religious symbols within Italian schools, which is both beyond our expertise and the theme of this book, see Cavana, "Modelli di laicità nelle società pluraliste"; and in particular Luzzatto, *Il crocifisso di stato.*

4. In France, "on the basis of the two laws for the secularization of public schools approved at the end of the nineteenth century (1882 and 1886), all religious teaching and symbols in public schools were outlawed.... Teaching roles in public schools were given exclusively to secular personnel and all teachers were given the requirement of strict neutrality, which from those times has gradually expanded to all state employees, who today have a strict ban on displaying, even in subtle ways, their religious beliefs in the workplace.... The approval of law n. 2004/228 on March 15, 2004 ... introduced in public schools a ban on wearing 'symbols or clothes through which students visibly display their religious beliefs'" (Cavana, "Modelli di laicità nelle società pluraliste"). On the question of the veil in French schools see Buruma, *Taming the Gods*, 112–15.

5. *Corriere della Sera*, May 5, 2006.

6. *Il Giornale*, May 19, 2013; *la Repubblica* (Firenze), March 27, 2013.

7. Examined in more detail below in chapter 5.

8. Exodus 20:1–6, emphasis added. All Biblical citations from the New Revised Standard Version.

9. Exodus 34:11–14, emphasis added.

10. For example, "in Japan, monotheism is often criticized as the cause of wars, conflicts, and the destruction of the environment," while polytheism and animism are seen by many as a solution to these problems. It is also interesting that Ken Sakamura, a computer engineer working on the creation of a "ubiquitous network society," associates his own model with the image of the "Japanese multitudinous gods": what he has in mind is thus a polytheism of the web and of virtual reality, which posits into the future the traditional "web" of *kami* found throughout the territory of Japan (Kohara, "Discourses and Realpolitik on Monotheism and Polytheism"). See also Bittarello, "Western Suspicion of Polytheism," 78.

CHAPTER TWO

1. I refer to the meaning that this category has in Jan Assmann's studies: see in particular *Cultural Memory and Early Civilization*, where "cultural memory" is the nexus of the three other types of memory, respectively defined as "mimetic," "communicative," and "of things."

2. A brief but very well-informed history of the nativity scene is Vermes, *The Nativity*; see also Lanzi and Lanzi, *Il presepe e i suoi personaggi*, esp. 10–50. A detailed historical/anthropological interpretation of the Christmas nativity scene can be found in Bettini, *Il presepio*.

3. On the nativity scene of Greccio see St. Bonaventure, *Legenda maior*, 10, 7; Lanzi and Lanzi, *Il presepe e i suoi personaggi*, 24, 41; as well as Bettini, *Il presepio*, 78–83.

4. See Rank, *The Myth of the Birth of the Hero*, with the observations of Freud, *L'uomo Mosé e la religione del monoteismo [Moses and Monotheism]*, esp. 340–44; Bettini and Borghini, *Il bambino e l'eletto*. For the medieval period Pörsken and Pörsken, "Die Geburt des Helden in Mittelhochdeutschen Epen und Epischen Stoffen des Mittelalters."

5. Luke 2:7; Matthew 2:13–18.

6. The grotto as the place of birth is mentioned in the *Infancy Gospel of James*, 18+. See Bettini, *Il presepio*, 8–15.

7. Luke 2: 8–20.

8. Matthew 2:1–12.

9. There are numerous interpretations; see Vermes, *The Nativity,* 109–14; Bettini, *Il presepio,* 56–70.

10. See John of Hildesheim, *Historia trium regum.*

CHAPTER THREE

1. See the famous essay by Lévi-Strauss, "Santa Claus Burned as a Heretic."

2. Klotz, "Sigillaria."

3. Bettini, *Lar familiaris.*

4. Wissowa, "Compitalia."

CHAPTER FOUR

1. Hug, "Lararium." See also a detailed examination of the documentation in Giacobello, *Larari pompeiani,* esp. 54–58. The term "lararium" first comes into use during the imperial age of Rome.

2. Orr, "Roman Domestic Religion," p. 1569; Tram Tan Tinh, "Lares," also has numerous reproductions of images of the *Lares,* 97ff. In some cases, the Lar is also wearing a kind of scarf that falls down the sides along the arms and hips: this piece of clothing is difficult to identify (Orr, 1569; Tram Tan Tinh, 211). In a fragment from the comedy *Tunicularia,* the poet Gnaeus Naevius describes the scene of a painter painting some *Lares ludentes* during a moment when they are playing or dancing. See Ribbeck, *Scaenicae Romanorum poesis fragmenta,* 24, 99ff; and De Marchi, *Il culto privato di Roma antica,* 45–49.

3. Cicero, *Against Verres,* II, 4, 4.; Petronius, *Satyricon,* 29, 2. Making an offering of the first beard to the Lares was a typical ceremony for the passage from pueritia to adulthood. On the Lares, see Bettini, "Lar familiaris."

4. Suetonius, *Divus Augustus,* 7.

5. *Historia Augusta: Life of Marcus Aurelius,* 3, 5.

6. *Historia Augusta: Life of Alexander Severus,* 29, 2.

7. *Historia Augusta: Life of Alexander Severus,* 31, 4. See also Settis, *Severo Alessandro e i suoi Lari.*

CHAPTER FIVE

1. See Assmann, *Mosè l'egizio [Moses the Egyptian]*, esp. 18–84); *Non avrai altro Dio; The Price of Monotheism.* Assmann's research, as can easily be imagined, is located within a much broader field of study that goes far beyond this point. Along with his works cited here, one could also include those discussed by Versnel in "Three Greek Experiments in Oneness."

2. See above in chapter 1.

3. In Assman, *Non avrai altro Dio.*

4. Freud, *Moses and Monotheism.* Assmann's theories have also come under criticism: aside from those of an ideological or theological nature, to which Assmann himself has responded many times, see also, for example, Baines, *Egyptian Deities in Context.*

5. Assmann, *Mosè l'egizio [Moses the Egyptian]*, 16. Assmann also writes that "natural evidence is debunked as seduction [and] [...] the distinction between true and false refers, in its ultimate meaning, to the distinction between god and world" ("Polytheism," 29).

6. Gibbon writes: "Under these circumstances, Christianity offered itself to the world, armed with the strength of the Mosaic law, and delivered from the weight of its fetters. An exclusive zeal for the truth of religion and the unity of God was as carefully inculcated in the new as in the ancient system" (*The Decline and Fall of the Roman Empire*, 387).

7. Freud, *Moses and Monotheism*, had already noted this : "Belief in a single god inevitably gave birth to religious intolerance, unknown in the ancient world before that moment and for many years after as well" (349, our translation).

8. This difference had not escaped Voltaire's notice in his *Treatise on Tolerance*, chapters 7–8; see also Bonnet, "Comme des noeuds qui les unissaient tous ensemble."

9. Augé, *Génie du paganisme*, 116. Assmann writes: "In the 'pagan' societies, violence exists based upon the political principle of sovereignty, and is not related to questions of the divine: it is a question of power, not of truth" (*Le prix du monothéisme [The Price of Monotheism]*, 32, our translation).

10. Hume, *Natural History of Religion*, chapter IX.

11. *Catechism of the Catholic Church*, http://www.vatican.va/archive/ENG0015/__P7C.HTM. All quotation marks are original, emphasis ours.

12. *Catechism of the Catholic Church*, 2085, http://www.vatican.va/archive/ENG0015/__P7C.HTM.

13. *Catechism of the Catholic Church*, 2104, http://www.vatican.va/archive/ENG0015/__P7D.HTM. The sources are noted in the footnotes of the *Catechism* itself.

14. *Catechism of the Catholic Church*, 2105–2106, http://www.vatican.va/archive/ENG0015/__P7D.HTM.

CHAPTER SIX

1. Some of the affirmations of the *Catechism* in terms of religious freedom and coercion, contained for example in articles 2108–2109, may in fact be cause for a certain degree of confusion: "The right to religious liberty is neither a moral license to adhere to error, nor a supposed right to error [...]. The right to religious liberty can of itself be neither unlimited nor limited only by a "public order" conceived in a positivist or naturalist manner [...]."

2. Assmann, *Mosè l'egizio [Moses the Egyptian*, 74–75; Assmann, "Polytheism..

3. Dupont, "Conclusion. L'altérité incluse"; Huet and Valette-Cagnac, "Et si les Romains avaient inventé la Grèce?"

4. See introduction.

5. "The Story of Salih," in Imam Ibn Kathir, *Stories of the Prophets*, 61.

6. Bouchy, "Quand Je est l'autre," 221–22.

7. On the concept of "cultural intimacy," see Rubel and Rosman, *Translating Cultures*, 17.

8. Scheid, "Les temples de l'Altbachtal à Trêves: un 'sanctuaire national?'"

9. Herodotus, *Histories*, 4, 59; Plutarch, *De Iside et Osiride*, 62.

10. Assmann provides on the other hand an eminently historical explanation of this phenomenon, tied to concrete circumstances and necessities (*Mosè l'egizio [Moses the Egyptian]*, 75–79). The starting point would consist of the assimilation of the Sumerian pantheon by the

Akkadians, after which this practice would "evolve into a cultural technique shared by all populations in the context of foreign policy and the rights of different peoples." This type of explanation, though, ignores the structural characteristics of polytheistic religions, whose intrinsic pluralism automatically made them into open systems that were capable of intersection. Cultural systems exist even outside of cultural history. See also Assmann's comment: "intercultural theology became a concern of international law" ("Polytheism").

CHAPTER SEVEN

1. Josephus, *Against Apion,* 2, 237; see also *Antiquities of the Jews,* 4, 207.

2. Exodus, 22: 28: *theoùs mè kakologéseis;* similarly in the Vulgate: *diis non detrahes.*

3. See Propp, "Exodus 19–40," 7, 262. Propp's exact translation of the Hebrew text is: "Deity don't curse, and a leader among your people don't execrate." The meaning of *elohim* in this context is debatable: given the presence of the other key term of the precept, *nasi,* which implicates a royal designation, the tendency is to give *elohim* the human meaning of "judge." The Greek translation appears "surprising," though understandable, if we consider the Egyptian religious milieu within which the translator was working (Propp).

4. Philo, *On the Life of Moses,* 2, 205; see also his *On the Special Laws,* 2, 53. The emperor Julian (*Against the Galileans,* 2, 238 D) would also make an appeal to the precept found in Exodus, according to the spirit found in the Greek translation, in order to accuse the Christians of also having ignored the Hebrew laws in terms of respect toward common gods, whom they not merely neglected, but also cursed.

5. On the extraordinary "variability" of the concept expressed by *theós* see also the long note in von Harnack (*Lehrbuch der Dogmengeschichte,* I, 138–39). Gibbon, following the work of Reland, calls attention to the "respect owed to the name of God" as a way to question the plausibility of the Edict of Omar, by which the books of the Library of Alexandria were supposedly put to flame (*The Decline and Fall,* chapter 51).

6. See Lang: "in Judaism, Christianity, and Islam, the unique god does not have a proper name or has only hints of one (as in Judaism).

The name of the Hebrew god, which modern research [...] renders as *Yahwe,* is substituted with "God," "Holy," "Eternal," and so forth. Even Allah simply means 'the God,'" ("Monotheismus," 149, our translation). In the cases in which the divine is called "Lord," "Eternal," "Highness," one proceeds by means of antonomasia, as the ancient rhetors would have said, by making an epithet take on the function of a proper name.

7. Minucius Felix, *Octavius,* 18.

8. In a recent Turkish translation of the Gospel, the use of "Allah" to render "God the Father" (alongside the removal of the phrase "son of God" for Jesus), raised heavy criticism among Christians; while in Malay, the Christian use of the name "Allah" to indicate God, despite a four-hundred-year tradition, led to a situation where "Islamic extremists accused the Catholic Church of usurping the name of their God, burnt down churches, confiscated Bibles, threatened newspapers, and brought legal charges against the Catholic leadership" (*Vatican Insider,* May 21, 2012; *Tempi,* June 29, 2013). On the other side, the English translations of the Koran tend to retain the word "Allah" as the name of the Muslim God, rather than the word "God," while many online documents can be found that insist that one cannot translate "God" as "Allah," and vice versa, demonstrating the fact that this opinion is strongly held.

9. See Bortone, *I gesuiti alla corte di Pechino,* 141–45; Martins do Vale, *Entre a cruz e o dragão,* 128–31; and especially Brockey, *Journey to East,* 84–89. For a philosophical comparison between the "sky" in Chinese culture and the Christian "God," see Gernet, *Chine et Christianisme,* 263–33 (in particular the inspired paragraph dedicated to the influence of language on the configuration of thought both in Western and Chinese people, seen as the source of many of Matteo Ricci's misunderstandings).

10. Scaliger, *Prima Scaligeriana, Nusquam antehac Edita,* 59: "Grammatica." An additional curiosity worth recalling is that Scaliger himself, while cataloging the European linguistic matrices (those languages that gave birth to many others) used precisely the noun "god" as an example: "sunto [...] quattuor haec verba, Deus, θεός, Godt, Boge, notae quattuor maiorum matricum, Latinae, Graecae, Theutonicae, Sclavonicae" (119ff).

CHAPTER EIGHT

1. Bettini, *Vertere*, 88–121; Bettini, *Interpretatio Romana*, 29–39.

2. As I have written elsewhere, according to the Roman point of view, translation of a foreign language was not a limited action, the way it is for us: it falls underneath the broader category of reformulations of a given phrase by different words. The Romans could say *interpretari* or *vertere* (the other word that corresponds more or less to our "translate") either about a phrase in a foreign language "translated" into the language of Rome, or a Latin phrase reproposed with other words, but still in Latin. See Bettini, *Vertere*, 117–21.

3. Tacitus, *The History*, 4, 84, 5.

4. On the Greek side, Plutarch, in his attempt to identify the Roman Picus and Faun with different Greek deities, used the term *proseikázein*, "assimilate through conjecture." I have investigated the specific value of *interpretatio* (an expression often used indiscriminately in studies of ancient religions), as well as some of the philological and anthropological aspects connected to this question, to a greater extent in Bettini, "*Interpretatio Romana:* Category or Conjecture?"

5. I am referring to Jakobson's 1959 essay "On Linguistic Aspects of Translation," in which the author uses this expression. See also Calabrese, "Lo strano caso dell'equivalenza imperfetta."

6. Arnobius, *Adversus Nationes*, 3, 32.

CHAPTER NINE

1. Saddington, "Roman Soldiers, Local Gods, and Interpretatio Romana in Roman Germany;" see also chapter 6.

2. Arnobius, *Adversus Nationes*, 2, 73.

3. Arnobius, *Adversus Nationes*, 2, 73.

4. On the question of the introduction of the worship of Apollo into Rome, see Wissowa, *Religion und Kultus der Römer*, 293–94.

5. Paper, *The Deities Are Many*, 125–26, our translation.

6. Tertullian, *The Prescription Against Heretics*, 7 and 14. This work is a genuine deprecation of the *curiositas* (defined as *restless* by Tertullian

because it stimulates study and research) that is considered a catalyst for error and heresy.

7. See Filoramo, "Tra coscienza e comunità."

8. The Catholic sphere witnessed a rise in this interest after the promulgation of the Encyclical *Nostra aetate* in 1965; without a doubt, though, the events of the past decades, from the Twin Towers to the exponential increase in global migration, make this mutual availability ever more essential.

9. During the Sunday Angelus on August 10, 2013, Pope Francis, just after the end of the month of Ramadan, offered "a greeting to Muslims throughout the world," calling them "our brothers," and adding: "my wishes are that Christians and Muslims will make the effort to promote mutual respect, especially through the education of future generations" (*Il Mattino,* August 11, 2013, emphasis added, our translation).

10. A city councillor from the Italian Northern League Party, Giuseppe Fornoni, after using the adjective "Muslim" as an insult toward the Minister of Integration Cécile Kyenge, used the following words as a justification: "You have to understand that I am a complete Catholic. I am Catholic first and foremost, you see? I am also a husband and a father, sure, but above all I am a Catholic" (*Il Giorno,* August 8, 2013, our translation).

CHAPTER TEN

1. Lang, "Monotheismus," 149.

2. See the chapter "La gloire des cités" in Albert-Llorca, *Les vierges miraculeuses,* 87–133. This work is also helpful on the question of the relationship—itself rather "polytheistic"—between the multiplicity of the images of the various Virgins, experienced as independent beings, and the uniqueness of the Virgin Mary herself.

3. "The class of deity" is the designation given by Nevling Porter in *One God or Many?;* on the question of the intrinsic, and in some ways inevitable, "polytheistic" tendencies within monotheistic religions, see Lang, "Monotheismus," 154–56, and the intriguing conclusions drawn by Bittarello, "Western Suspicion of Polytheism," esp. 76–77.

CHAPTER ELEVEN

1. https://www.merriam-webster.com/dictionary/tolerance.

2. See, for example, Seneca, *Epistulae,* 31, 7 and 66, 13; Cicero, *Paradoxa Stoicorum,* 27; etc.

3. See, for example, Cicero, *De officiis,* 1, 79; Sallustius, *De coniuratione Catilinae,* 53, 3; Virgil, *Aeneis,* 8, 515; Tacitus, *Annales,* 13, 48; Sallustius, *Bellum Iugurthinum,* 22, 3; etc.

4. d'Holbach, *La contagion sacrée* (see chapter: "De la tolérance").

5. Cyprian, *De bono patientiae,* 6; Augustine, *Ad catholicos epistula contra Donatistas,* 1, 5; *Epistulae,* 44, 11; *Contra litteras Petiliani Donatistae,* 1, 28; *De baptismo,* 7, 103; etc. See also the summary by Schreiner in *Toleranz,* 445–494; Bejczy, "Tolerantia."

6. St. Augustine, *Epistulae,* 85, 24; Luke 14:21–23. Schreiner writes, "Augustine did not view resorting to force against heretics as being *intolerantia,* but as a legitimate religious reaction to the violent provocations made by the Donatists" (*Toleranz,* 453).

7. Zagorin, *How the Idea of Religious Toleration Came to the West*; Zagorin, "Religious Toleration." See also d'Holbach, *La contagion sacrée,* 116–44.

8. Globalization and immigration in fact put into contrast communities that are not only animated by different religious faiths, but also by different ways of conceiving the boundaries of religions. See Filoramo, "Tra coscienza e comunità"; on the criticisms that are sometimes made of tolerance (seen as a form of cultural weakness), see Buruma, *Taming the Gods,* 108–10.

9. Schreiner, "Toleranz," 446, cites "schwammig" from Mitscherlich, *Toleranz,* 7 ("spongy": our translation). Even today, the term "tolerance" can be understood both as a religious freedom conceded to a minority by a dominant religion, and as such, potentially revocable, and as religious freedom in a fuller sense, and as such included amongst fundamental human rights. See Zagorin, "Religious Toleration," 689–90.

10. According to Crick in "Toleration and Tolerance in Theory and Practice," "toleration" implies "disapproval or disagreement coupled with an unwillingness to take action against those who are viewed with disfavor," etc.

11. *Catechism of the Catholic Church* 2015–2106, http://www.vatican.va/archive/ENG0015/__P7D.HTM.

12. See introduction.

13. On "religious intolerance" in antiquity, see appendix 1 below.

CHAPTER TWELVE

1. Pironti, "Gli dèi e le dèe dei Greci," 518–54.

2. Cicero, *De natura deorum,* 3, 39 and 47.

3. Porphyrion, *Commentarius in Horatii epistulas,* 1, 10, 49: *Vacuna in Sabinis dea, quae sub incerta specie est formata. Hanc quidam Bellonam, alii Minervam, alii Dianam putant.*

4. This is the phenomenon that Assmann ("Polytheism," 25) calls "hyphenating gods." Our formulation has the advantage of moving the phenomenon from the realm of orthography to that of linguistics.

5. On the cult-like characteristics of foreign gods, see Van Doren, "Peregrina Sacra." On the ritual aspects of the cult of Hercules, which for the Romans were celebrated "according to the Greek rites" see Dumézil, *Archaic Roman Religion,* 378–379.

6. Servius, *Commentarius in Aeneidem,* 2, 351; Macrobius, *Saturnalia,* 3, 9, 2; see also Pliny, *Naturalis historia,* 2, 28; Dumézil, *Archaic Roman Religion,* 369–70. On the cult-like characteristics of the *evocatae* divinities, as seen as *sacra peregrina,* see Van Doren, "Peregrina Sacra."

7. On *fas,* see Benveniste, *Dictionary of Indo-European Concepts and Society;* Bettini, "Mos, mores e mos maiorum," 257–58.

8. Arnobius, *Adversus nationes,* 3, 4 (= fr. 12 Beck-Walter: see Beck and Walter, *Die frühen römischen Historiker,* pp. 146–47]), our translation.

9. Nietzsche, *The Anti-Christ,* 19.

10. The multiple forms of worship known as syncretic religions that can be found throughout the world, and which certainly do not receive any approval from official hierarchies, fall outside the focus of this work.

11. See also the other texts cited in Assmann, *The Price of Monotheism,* 100–3.

CHAPTER THIRTEEN

1. See Rüpke, *La religione dei Romani [The Religion of the Romans]*, pp. 32–33 and especially Scheid, *Les dieux, l'État e l'individu*, pp. 143–151.

2. Cicero, *De legibus*, 2, 19.

3. See chapter 12 (Honos, Fides, Mens, etc.).

4. Suetonius, *Augustus*, 91.

5. Festus, *De significatione verborum*, 268; Lindsay, our translation; see also Van Doren, "Peregrina sacra."

6. Cicero, *De haruspicum responso*, 27; *In Verrem*, 5, 87; etc.

7. Seneca, *Epistulae ad Lucilium*, 120, 4; *Naturales quaestiones*, 5, 16, 4; etc. Just like the people who made foreign words "citizens," Cicero's Cato gave "citizenship" to philosophy, a field of study that was still at that time "foreign" to Rome (*De finibus*, 3, 40), Columella (*De agricultura*, 1, 1, 12) gave it to the science of agriculture, which had been the heritage of the Greeks up to that time, and Quintilian (*Institutio oratoria*, 8, 1, 3) hoped that an oratory that was truly Roman would come about, and not just one that had been "made a citizen." By the term "cognitive metaphor," we mean "metaphorically defined mental models...schematic cognitive representations that constitute the more-or-less shared basis of and motivation for much of what people say, think, and do," that "achieve a way of defining not only how a society's different symbolic activities across different domains of practice cohere together into a unified, totalizing, and so natural-seeming signifying order, but also how they can be perceived as such by those who live according to this order" (Short, "Metaphor," 60).

8. John Scheid wrote on the topic of Roman gods as "citizens" with particular clarity in many of his works: see, for example, "Numa et Jupiter ou les dieux citoyens de Rome"; "Politique et religion dans la Rome antique"; *Les dieux, l'État et l'individu*, 166. See also the earlier work by Michels, "Review of K. Latte, *Römische Religionsgeschichte*" In order to define this characteristic of the Roman gods, Scheid uses an expression from Minucius Felix, *dii municipes* (*Octavius*, 6, *deos colere municipes*), which he rightly translates as "dieux concitoyens" ("Politique et religion dans la Rome antique"; *Les dieux, l'État et l'individu*, 166).

On the indissoluble link between "city" and "religion" in Rome, see Scheid, *Les dieux, l'État et l'individu*, esp. 95–120.

9. Cicero, *De natura deorum*, 3, 39; cfr. Pauli Festus 13 Lindsay; Josephus, *Contra Apionem*, 2, 25, 251.

10. Cicero, *De legibus*, 2, 26.

11. Ovid, *Metamorphoses*, 1, 167ff. See also Perfigli, "Politeismo."

12. Augustine, *De civitate dei*, 6, 4, 11 s. (= fr. 5 Cardauns).

13. Tertullian himself, turning Roman religious categories to his own advantage, had sarcastically noted that "for you [gentiles], god depends on human judgment. A god who does not make himself liked by men will no longer be god: it is man who must show that he is well-disposed towards a god!" (*Apologeticus*, 5, 1; cfr. 10, 13, our translation).

14. Ovid, *Fastorum libri*, 3, 819.

15. See Bettini, "Missing Cosmogonies."

16. Arnobius, *Adversus nationes*, 7, 32, 9. The day on which a temple was consecrated was of great importance in Rome; see Servius, *Commentarius in Aeneidem*, 8, 601: "for the Romans, nothing was as solemn as the day of consecration" (our translation).

17. Cicero, *De natura deorum*, 3, 2, our translation.

18. There was thus no reason for amazement (which was how Augustine reacted) if in Rome "you see how their wise men, whom they call philosophers, have different schools but the same temples" (Augustine, *De vera religione*, 1).

19. See Bettini, *Contro le radici*.

20. See Buruma, *Taming the Gods*, 114–15, on British multiculturalism as compared to the model of national uniformity that is preferred in France.

CHAPTER FOURTEEN

1. Oxford English Dictionary, entry for "Polytheism."

2. See note 14, below.

3. See Borgeaud and Prescendi, *Religioni antiche*, 22–23; on the "religious categories" of the Romans, see Scheid, *Les dieux, l'État et l'individu*, 97–99.

4. Whoever practices *tò polýtheon* resembles the creatures who slither along the ground, and will be punished for this sin; moreover, more than once those who worship many gods are compared to the children of prostitutes, whom Deuteronomy 23:2 excludes from the divine *ekklesía.* Last, those who do not recognize themselves as children of a single father, but who hop from one god to another, demonstrate that they do not love peace, and provoke constant wars and revolts. See Philo, *De mutatione nominum,* 205; *De opificio,* 171; *De ebrietate,* 108–110; *De confusione linguarum,* 42, 144; *De migratione Abrahami,* 69; *Quis rerum divinarum heres,* 169; *De decalogo,* 65; *De fuga et inventione,* 114; *De virtutibus,* 21; 221; *De praemiis et poenis,* 162. The latter statement by Philo sounds rather paradoxical considering the historical perspective of how much conflict in the other direction was provoked (by the two successive monotheisms) by the claim of being the true children of the unique Father. In Aeschylus, *Supplices,* 424, we can already find the adjective *polýtheos,* but used metaphorically in reference to a place in which many gods are worshiped.

5. Pseudo-Justin, *Cohortatio ad Graecos,* 15, 1 (Migne, *Patrologia Graeca,* VI, 269–70). For the chronology and the authenticity of this work, see Lietzmann, "Iustinus der Martyrer"; Puech, *Histoire de la littérature grecque chrétienne,* II:215–17. Other similar references from Christian texts include *polytheéo,* "I love many gods," *polýtheos,* "who loves many gods," *polytheótes,* "the religion of many gods," *polytheïa,* "multiplicity of gods," (often used in conjunction with *dáimones, diábolos,* etc.), etc (from Lampe, *A Patristic Greek Lexicon,* 116).

6. Bodin, *De la Demonomanie des Sorciers,* 29. In Cardinal Ercole Cato's translation into Italian, this phrase is rendered as "il Politheismo è un dritto Atheismo" (Cato, *Demonomania de gli stregoni,* 64). Purchas, *His Pilgrimage,* first Part, first Book, ch. IX, 49; see Schmidt, "Les polythéismes. Dégénérescence ou Progrès?," 69–70n3. In spite of Schmidt's research, there is still a certain degree of confusion amongst scholars about the history and usage of "polytheism" and the other related terms: Bittarello, in her otherwise excellent work, claims that the term was originally used by Eastern Christian elites to describe the Greco-Roman religion, after which it would get "picked up" (?) by

Philo; Frevel, in *Beyond Monotheism?*, goes so far as to attribute the use of the term to Tertullian (?) and claims that in the modern period it was introduced as an antonym to "monotheism" (??).

7. Lang, "Monotheismus," 150.

8. More, *An Explanation of the Grand Mystery of Godliness*, 62. MacDonald reconstructs in detail the events leading to the birth of this expression against the backdrop of the many "-isms" that would populate the theological and philosophical debates of the seventeenth century ("Deuteronomy and the Meaning of 'Monotheism,'" 4–7).

9. More, *Apocalypsis Apocalypseos*, 84. See Lang, "Monotheismus," 150–60; Sabbatucci, *Monoteismo*, 9; Filoramo, *Che cos'è la religione*, 186–89.

10. "Pagani autem ea ratione dicti sunt, quia Christi non sunt milites: siquidem in iure hi sunt pagani, qui non militant, et in pagis et vicis suis munera subeunt" (Alciato, *Andreae Alciati Iureconsulti Mediolanensis ΠΑΡΕΡΓΩΝ iuris libri tres*, Liber primus, Capitulum XIII, 16).

11. Baronio, *Martyrologium Romanum restitutum*, 61.

12. On *paganus* and its various interpretations, see Appendix 2 below.

13. The words "idolater" and "idolatry" show an incidence of haplology compared to the original Greek words, precisely in the loss of the syllable *-lo-* before the *-la-* (idololatria → idolatry).

14. See expressions like "Idolatry not only refers to false pagan worship," *Catechism of the Catholic Church*, 2113; or "the persecution of Christians by the Roman government [...] was due to their refusal to participate in the idolatrous imperial cult" (Zagorin, "Religious Toleration," 690). The latter statement, coming from a scholarly text, is particularly surprising, though it is not an isolated case.

15. See the discussion by Barbu, *Idole, idolâtre, idolâtrie*. The inconstancy and vanity of Gentile images is a detail that was specifically highlighted by Christians when they spoke of *éidola* or of *idola*. "When you were pagans (*ethnikói*)—St. Paul would say—you were led by *éidola* (= vain images) with no voices (*áphona*)"; just as Augustine did not hesitate to call the images worshiped by those who believed in many, and false, gods, *inutilia simulacra* (Paul, *Ad Corinthios*, 1, 12, 2; Augustine, *De*

civitate dei, 6, *Praefatio*). Our study, looking exclusively at the origin of the word "idol" and its original semantics, obviously does not include the immense subsequent popularity that this term would have, or the countless transformations of its meaning. In this vast ocean of questions and answers, we mention Halbertal and Margalit, *Idolatry.*

16. *Thesaurus linguae latinae,* VI/1, 133–134. Alongside *simulacra,* Augustine (in *Locutiones in Pentateuchum,* 2, 138) would use the expression *facticii dei.* For the Romance examples, see the Provençal *fachiz* and the Spanish *hechizo,* which mean "artistic" but also "spell"; the Portuguese *feitiço,* from which comes *feiticeiro,* "witch-doctor," the Italian terms *fattura* (both "craftsmanship" and "evil eye") and *fattucchiera* ("witch"), together with the Spanish *hechicero,* which has the same meaning. See Meyer-Lübke, *Romanisches Etymologisches Lexicon,* 3132.

17. De Brosses, *Du culte des dieux fétiches.* See also Iacono, *Le fétichisme.*

18. The usage of these terms in anthropology and in historical-religious studies has, however, been quite unfortunate. Along these lines, Marcel Mauss ("Année Sociologique," 1907, cited in Iacono, *Le fétichisme,* 116) spoke expressly about the "immense malentendu" that hides behind words like "fétiche" and "fétichisme," words that are misunderstood because of the "aveugle obéissance à l'usage colonial, à les langues franques parlées par les Européens, à la culture occidentale."

19. Augustine, *De civitate dei,* Preface.

20. The use of "paganism" as a category of abomination is still alive and well in the sermons of televangelists in the US (see Kirsch, *God Against the Gods,* 6–14). Following September 11, 2001, Jerry Falwell even included "pagans" amongst those who "had made it possible for all of this to happen" (along with homosexuals, feminists, and abortion-rights activists, obviously). As Nietzsche wrote in *Human, All Too Human,* 1, 531: "He who lives by fighting with an enemy has an interest in the preservation of the enemy's life."

21. In Cagliari, Pope Francis condemned the "god of money" (*la Repubblica,* 22 September 2013) and during the homily of Santa Marta condemned the "goddess of bribes" (*Corriere della sera,* 8 November 2013); in Paris, Benedict XVI—explicitly calling idolatry a "plague," exactly like John Chrysostom had—implored everyone to take

refuge from the "idols" of power and money (*Il Giornale,* 14 September 2008); etc.

22. Cameron offers a different opinion in *The Last Pagans of Rome,* where he lists a series of descriptions ("pagan literature," "pagan reaction," etc.) that he finds particularly inappropriate and potential causes for misunderstanding; nonetheless, he prefers to use the adjective "pagan" as "the simplest, the most familiar and most appropriate term" to define his object of study, while making the additional observation that other alternatives for "paganism"—such as "polytheism"—don't much improve matters.

23. A brief list of other characteristics of polytheism compared to monotheism can be found in Assmann, "Polytheism"; a rather longer, very detailed comparative chart is in Bittarello, *Western Suspicion of Polytheism,* 83–84.

24. Augé uses the expression "intellectual availability" when speaking about African gods (*Genie de paganisme,* 182ff). On the intellectual originality of polytheism, see our introduction.

CHAPTER FIFTEEN

1. Dodds, *The Greeks and the Irrational,* 229.

2. See Paper, *The Deities Are Many,* 106. According to Bittarello the obstacle in the path of accepting polytheism within the West is actually an epistemological barrier: it would represent a threat to an entire set of concepts that are implicitly considered positive, such as "unity," "totality," "homogeneity," "stability" ("Western Suspicion of Polytheism, 78–79).

3. Lang, "Monotheismus," 148–49.

4. Severi, "Autorités sans auteurs;" see also Assmann, *Religion and Cultural Memory,* esp. 63–121.

5. This episode is recounted in Buruma, *Taming the Gods,* 120–21, *our emphasis.*

6. Borgeaud and Prescendi, *Religioni antiche,* 21–35; Scheid, *Les dieux, l'État et l'individu,* 165–74. It seems paradoxical, though, that the university field of study called "History of Religions" in Italian universities today has become a subsection of an interdisciplinary grouping called

"Science of the Book," as if all religions must, by definition, have a book. Someone really should correct this mistake.

7. Tertullian, *Apologeticus,* 18, 1ff. For a more thorough examination of this question, see Bettini, *Vertere,* 189–202.

8. Paul, *Digesta,* 22, 4, 1.

9. For the latter meaning of *instrumentum* see *Thesaurus linguae latinae,* VII/2, 2014, 22ff, entry: "Instrumentum."

10. Bettini, *Vertere,* 189–260.

11. Herodotus, *Historiae,* 2, 53.

12. Josephus, *Contra Apionem,* 2, 36, 251.

13. See also chapter 13.

14. *Catechism of the Catholic Church,* 105, https://www.vatican.va/archive/ENG0015/__PP.HTM, our emphasis.

15. Benedetti has written many insightful pages on this subject (*Disumane lettere,* 119–27).

APPENDIX A

1. Garnsey, "Religious Tolerance in Classical Antiquity."

2. Cassius Dio, *Roman History,* 52, 36, 1ff.

3. Arnobius, *Adversus nationes,* 3, 2: *si vobis divina res cordi est, cur alios nobiscum neque deos colitis neque adoratis nec cum vestris gentibus communia sacra miscetis et religionum coniungitis ritus?*

4. Buruma, *Taming the Gods,* 75.

5. As reported by Livy, *The History of Rome,* 39, 18, 7. See also *CIL* I2 2, 581. See Weissenborn, *Ab urbe condita,* p. 8.

6. Apuleius, *Metamorphoses,* 9, 14, 5.

7. On whether or not we can use the category of religious tolerance/intolerance for the ancient world, Garnsey's reflections in "Religious Tolerance in Classical Antiquity" are still of great interest; unfortunately the essays on antiquity found in Neusner and Chilton (*Religious Tolerance in World Religions,* 31–130), despite being of the best intentions, are marred by inaccuracies and misunderstandings, and have more of an amateur than a scholarly quality. The theme of "freedom of religion" in Rome, and of the related control over religion, has often been taken up by academics, and with particular clarity by Scheid in "Politique et

religion dans la Rome antique." From a different perspective, see the wide-ranging reflections found in Beard, North, and Price, *Religions of Rome*, 1:211–44, and previous to that in North, "Religious Toleration in Roman Republic," particularly about the *affaire* of the *Bacchanalia*. See also an excellent summary in Borgeaud and Prescendi, *Religions antiques*, 134–40. On the meaning of religious repression in Rome, see again Scheid, *Les dieux, l'État et l'individu*, 153–64. On the non-existence of a list of authorized religions in Rome, see Rüpke, *The Religion of the Romans*, 42. On ancient religious satire see Soler, "La déesse Syrienne." On whether or not one can use the contemporary concept of "fundamentalism" when speaking about the ancient world, see the essays in Barceló, *Religiöser Fundamentalismus in der römischen Kaiserzeit*.

8. Livy, *The History of Rome*, 4, 30, 9–11. This is different from the case of 25, 1, 2 and 36, 16, 8–9, where we find the repression of foreign *ritus*, or rather the way of "performing" religion, not of foreign gods. Francesca Prescendi is currently working on this subject, and I have taken these insights from her while waiting to read the finished version of her research.

9. On these subjects, we can recommend Garnsey, "Religious Tolerance in Classical Antiquity"; Beatrice, "L'intolleranza dei cristiani nei confronti dei pagani"; Paschoud, "L'intolleranza cristiana vista dai pagani"; Drake, "Lambs into Lions;" and especially Filoramo, "Tra coscienza e comunità" and "Sono le religioni monoteistiche (in) tolleranti?"

10. Stroumsa, *La formazione dell'identità cristiana*, 162, cited in Filoramo, "Sono le religioni monoteistiche (in)tolleranti?," our translation.

11. Beatrice, "L'intolleranza dei cristiani nei confronti dei pagani," 9.

12. Tertullian, *Apologeticus*, 24, 6; *Ad Scapulam*, 2, 1.

13. On this ambivalence, see especially the reflections of Filoramo, "Sono le religioni monoteistiche (in)tolleranti?"

APPENDIX B

1. Mohrmann, "Encore une fois: paganus"; Athanassiadi and Frede, *Pagan Monotheism in Late Antiquity*, 1–16 and n4; Cameron, *The Last Pagans of Rome*, 14–15.

2. Cameron, *The Last Pagans of Rome.*

3. Mohrmann, "Encore une fois: paganus." Mohrmann's interpretation was preceded by at least one excellent study (which she appears to have not known about) by Boscherini, "Paganus." A detailed presentation of the materials can be found under the heading of *paganus* in the *Thesaurus linguae Latinae,* X/1, 81, 3–27, in which there is also the primary bibliography on the subject; we add to this list Colpe, "Die Ausbildung des Heidenbegriffs von Israel zur Apologetik und das Zweideutigwerden des Christentums"; see also, in general, the discussion in Cameron, *The Last Pagans of Rome.*

BIBLIOGRAPHY

Albert-Llorca, M. *Les vierges miraculeuses. Légendes et rituels.* Paris: Gallimard, 2002.

Alciato, A. *Andreae Alciati Iureconsulti Mediolanensis ΠΑΡΕΡΓΩΝ iuris libri tres.* Lugduni apud Heredes S. Vincentii, 1538.

Arnobius. *Adversus Nationes.* Translated by Archdeacon Hamilton Bryce, LL. D., and Hugh Campbell, M. A. In *Anti-Nicene Fathers,* Vol. 6. ed. Philip Schaff. https://ccel.org/ccel/schaff/anf06/anf06.xii.iii.iii.xxxii.html.

Assmann, Jan. *Cultural Memory and Early Civilization: Writing, Remembrance, and Political Imagination.* Cambridge, UK: Cambridge University Press, 2011.

———. *Moses the Egyptian: The Memory of Egypt in Western Monotheism.* Cambridge, MA: Harvard University Press, 1997.

———. *Non avrai altro Dio. Il monoteismo e il linguaggio della violenza.* Bologna: Il Mulino, 2007.

———. "Polytheism." In *Religions of the Ancient World,* edited by S. I. Johnston, 17–31. Cambridge, MA: Harvard University Press, 2004.

———. *The Price of Monotheism.* Stanford, CA: Stanford University Press, 2009.

———. *Religion and Cultural Memory.* Stanford, CA: Stanford University Press, 2006.

Athanassiadi, P., and M. Frede, eds. *Pagan Monotheism in Late Antiquity.* Oxford: Oxford University Press, 1999.

Augé, Marc. *Génie du paganisme.* Paris: Gallimard, 2008.

Augustine of Hippo. *De civitate dei.* Translated by Marcus Dodd. In *Nicene and Post-Nicene Fathers,* Vol. 2, ed. Philip Schaff. https://ccel.org/ccel/schaff/npnf102/npnf102.iv.html.

———. *Epistulae.* Translated by J. G. Cunningham. In *Nicene and Post-Nicene Fathers,* Vol. 1, ed. Philip Schaff. https://en.wikisource.org/wiki/Nicene_and_Post-Nicene_Fathers:_Series_I/Volume_I/Letters_of_St._Augustin/Letters_of_St._Augustin.

———. *On Chistian Doctrine.* Translated by J. F. Shaw. In *Nicene and Post-Nicene Fathers,* Vol. 2, ed. Philip Schaff. https://en.wikisource.org/wiki/Nicene_and_Post-Nicene_Fathers:_Series_I/Volume_II/On_Christian_Doctrine.

Baines, J. "Egyptian Deities in Context: Multiplicity, Unity, and the Problem of Change." In *One God or Many? Concepts of Divinity in the Ancient World,* edited by B. Nevling Porter, 9–78. Chebeague, ME: Casco Bay Assyriological Institute, 2000.

Barbu, D. "Idole, idolâtre, idolâtrie." In *Les représentations des dieux des autres.* Actes du Colloque FIGVRA, Toulouse, 9–11 décembre 2010, edited by C. Bonnet, A. Declerq and I. Slododzianek, 32–49. Siracusa: Sciascia, 2011.

Barceló, P., ed. *Religiöser Fundamentalismus in der römischen Kaiserzeit.* Stuttgart: Franz Steiner, 2010.

Baronio, C. *Martyrologium Romanum restitutum, Gregorii XIII jussu editum.* Rome: 1586.

Beard, M., J. North, and S. Price. *Religions of Rome,* Vol. I. Cambridge, UK: Cambridge University Press, 1998.

Beatrice, P. F. "L'intolleranza dei cristiani nei confronti dei pagani: un problema storiografico." In *L'intolleranza dei cristiani nei confronti dei pagani,* edited by P. F. Beatrice, 7–13. Bologna: Centro editoriale dehoniano, 1990.

Beck, F., and U. Walter. *Die frühen römischen Historiker, vol. I.* Stuttgart: Wissenschaftliche Buchgesellschaft, 2005.

Bejczy, I. "Tolerantia: A Medieval Concept." *Journal of the History of Ideas,* 58 (1997): 365–84.

Benedetti, C. *Disumane lettere. Indagini sulla cultura della nostra epoca.* Roma-Bari: Laterza, 2011.

Benveniste, Émile. *Dictionary of Indo-European Concepts and Society.* Chicago: HAU Press, 2016.

Bettini, Maurizio. "Ad negotia humana compositi. *L'agency humaine des dieux antiques.*" In *Les dieux d'Homère II. Anthropomorphisme,* edited by R. Gagné and Miguel Herrero de Jáuregui, Kernos Supplement 33, 261–76. Liège: Presses Universitaires de Liège, 2019.

———. *Contro le radici.* Bologna: Il Mulino, 2012.

———. *Il presepio: Antropologia e storia della cultura.* Torino: Einaudi, 2018.

———. "*Interpretatio Romana:* Category or Conjecture?" In *Dieux des grecs, dieux des romains,* edited by C. Bonnet, V. Pirenne-Delforge, and G. Pironti, 17–36. Brussels: Belgisch Historisch Instituut te Rome, 2016.

———. "Lar familiaris: un dio semplice." *Lares* 73 (2007): 533–51.

———. "Missing Cosmogonies. The Roman Case?" *Archiv für Religionsgeschichte* 13 (2011): 69–92.

———. "Mos, mores e mos maiorum. L'invenzione dei 'buoni costumi' nella cultura romana." In *Le orecchie di Hermes. Studi di antropologia e letterature classiche,* 241–92. Torino: Einaudi, 2000.

———. *Vertere. Un'antropologia della traduzione nella cultura antica.* Torino: Einaudi, 2012.

Bettini, M., and Borghini, A. "Il bambino e l'eletto. Logica di una peripezia culturale." *Materiali e discussioni per l'analisi dei testi classici* 3 (1979): 121–53.

Bittarello, Maria Beatrice. "Western Suspicion of Polytheism, Western Thought Structures, and Contemporary Pagan Polytheisms." *Journal of Religion in Europe* 3 (2010): 68–102.

Bodin, J. *De la Demonomanie des Sorciers.* Paris: chez Jacques du Puys, 1580.

Bonnet, C. "'Comme des noeuds qui les unissaient tous ensemble' (Voltaire). Le processus d'interpretatio en Phénicie à l'époque hellénistique." In *Comptes-rendus des séances,* 503–15. Paris: Académie des Inscriptions et Belles-Lettres, 2012.

Borgeaud, Philippe, and Francesca Prescendi, eds. *Religioni antiche.* Roma: Carocci, 2011.

Bortone, F. *I gesuiti alla corte di Pechino.* Roma: Desclée, 1969.
Boscherini, S. "Paganus." *Lingua nostra* 17 (1956): 101–7.
Bouchy, A. "Quand Je est l'autre. Altérité et identité dans la possession au Japon." *L'Homme* 153 (2000): 207–30.
Brockey, L.M. *Journey to East: The Jesuit Mission to China, 1579–1724.* Cambridge, MA: Harvard University Press, 2007.
Buruma, Ian. *Taming the Gods: Religion and Democracy on Three Continents.* Princeton, NJ: Princeton University Press, 2010.
Calabrese, O. "Lo strano caso dell'equivalenza imperfetta." *Sulla traduzione intersemiotica,* edited by N. Dusi and S. Neergard, 101–20. Milano: Bompiani, 2000.
Calasso, Roberto. *Literature and the Gods.* New York: Vintage, 2002.
Cameron, A. *The Last Pagans of Rome.* Oxford: Oxford University Press, 2011.
Cassius Dio. *Roman History.* 9 vols. Cambridge, MA: Harvard University Press, 1914–1927. https://penelope.uchicago.edu/Thayer/E/Roman/Texts/Cassius_Dio/home.html.
Cato, E., trans. *Demonomania de gli stregoni cioè furori et malie de demoni.* Translation of Jean Bodin, *De la Demonomanie des Sorciers.* Venetia: presso Aldo, 1592.
Cavana, Paolo. "Modelli di laicità nelle società pluraliste. La questione dei simboli religiosi nello spazio pubblico." *Osservatorio delle libertà e delle istituzioni religiose* 2 (April 2005). http://www.olir.it/areetematiche/73/documents/cavana_campobasso.pdf.
Cicero. *Against Verres.* In *The Orations of Marcus Tullius Cicero,* translated by C.D. Yonge. London: George Bell & Sons, 1903. http://data.perseus.org/citations/urn:cts:latinLit:phi0474.phi005.perseus-eng1:2.4.
Colpe, C. "Die Ausbildung des Heidenbegriffs von Israel zur Apologetik und das Zweideutigwerden des Christentums." In *Die Restauration der Götter,* edited by R. Faber and R. Schlesier, 61–87. Würzburg: Königshausen und Neumann, 1986.
Cotkin, George. "William James and the Cash-Value Metaphor." *Etc. A Review of General Semantics* 42 (April 1, 1985): 37–46.
Crick, B. "Toleration and Tolerance in Theory and Practice." *Government and Opposition: A Journal of Comparative Politics* 6 (1971): 144–71.

de Brosses, C. *Du culte des dieux fétiches, ou parallèle de l'ancienne religion de l'Égypte avec la religion actuelle de Nigritie.* N.p.: n.p., 1760.

De Marchi, A. *Il culto privato di Roma antica,* vol. I. Forlì: Victrix, 2003.

Detienne, Marcel. "Du polythéisme en général." *Classical Philology* 81 (1986): 47–55.

———. *Comparer l'incomparable.* Paris: Seuil, 2009.

d'Holbach, P.-H. *La contagion sacrée ou Histoire naturelle de la superstition.* Edited by J. P. Jackson. Paris: Coda, 2006.

Dodds, E. R. *The Greeks and the Irrational.* Oakland: University of California Press, 1966.

Drake, H. D. "Lambs into Lions: Explaining Early Christian Intolerance." *Past and Present* 153 (1996): 3–33.

Drob, S. L. "The Depth of the Soul: James Hillman's Vision of Psychology." *Journal of Humanistic Psychology* 39 (1999): 56–72.

Dumézil, Georges. *Archaic Roman Religion.* Baltimore: Johns Hopkins University Press, 1996.

Dupont, F. "Conclusion. L'altérité incluse." In *Façons de parler grec à Rome,* edited by F. Dupont and E. Valette-Cagnac, 255–77. Paris: Belin, 2005.

Faber, R., and R. Schlesier, eds. *Die Restauration der Götter.* Würzburg: Königshausen und Neumann, 1986.

Filoramo, G. *Che cos'è la religione. Temi, metodi e problemi.* Torino: Einaudi, 2004.

———. "Sono le religioni monoteistiche (in)tolleranti? Il caso del cristianesimo antico." In *Studium Sapientiae. Atti della Giornata di studio in onore di Giulia Sfameni Gasparro (January 28, 2011),* edited by A. Cosentino and M. Monaca, 113–25. Rubbettino: Soveria Minnelli, 2013.

———. "Tra coscienza e comunità. I confini della tolleranza nella storia del cristianesimo." *Humanitas* 62 (2007): 150–60.

Freud, Sigmund. *Moses and Monotheism.* London: Hogarth Press, 1939.

Frevel, C. "Beyond Monotheism? Some Remarks and Questions on Conceptualising Monotheism." *Biblical Studies, Verbum et Ecclesia* 34, no. 2 (2013). http://dx.doi.org/10.4102.

Funkenstein, Amos. "The Polytheism of William James." *Journal of the History of Ideas* 55, no. 1 (January 1994): 99–111.

Garnsey, P. "Religious Tolerance in Classical Antiquity." *Studies in Church History* 21 (1984): 1–27.

Gernet, J. *Chine et Christianisme. Action et réaction.* Paris: Gallimard, 1982.

Gibbon, E. *The Decline and Fall of the Roman Empire,* vol. II. New York: The Modern Library, 2013.

Gladigow, Burkhard. "Polytheism." In *The Brill Dictionary of Religion,* vol. III. Leiden-Boston: Brill, 2007.

Giacobello, F. *Larari pompeiani.* Milan: Led, 2008.

Halbertal, M., and A. Margalit. *Idolatry.* Cambridge, MA: Harvard University Press, 1992.

Hegel, G. W. F. "The Oldest Systematic Program of German Idealism." Translated by Diana Behler. https://control-society.livejournal.com/10718.html.

Heine, Heinrich. "The Gods in Exile." In *The Prose Writings of Heinrich Heine.* Frankfurt: Outlook Verlag, 2020.

Heinrichs, A. "'Full of Gods': Nietzsche on Greek Polytheism and Culture." In *Nietzsche and Antiquity,* edited by P. Bishop, 115–37. Rochester, NY: Camden House, 2004.

Hillman, J. "On the Necessity of Abnormal Psychology." In *Eranos Jahrbuch* 43, edited by A. Portman and R. Ritsema, 91–135. Leiden: Brill, 1974.

Historia Augusta: Life of Marcus Aurelius. Translated by David Magie. Cambridge, MA: Loeb Classical Library, 1921. https://penelope.uchicago.edu/Thayer/E/Roman/Texts/Historia_Augusta/Marcus_Aurelius/1*.html.

Historia Augusta: Life of Alexander Severus. Translated by David Magie. Cambridge, MA: Loeb Classical Library, 1921. https://penelope.uchicago.edu/Thayer/E/Roman/Texts/Historia_Augusta/Severus_Alexander/2*.html.

Huet, V., and E. Valette-Cagnac, eds. "Et si les Romains avaient inventé la Grèce?" *Mètis* 3 (2005).

Hug, A. "Lararium." In *Realencyclopädie der classischen Altertumswissenschaft,* vol. XII, coll. 794–795. Berlin-Heidelberg: Springer-Verlag, 1992.

Hume, David. *Dialogues and Natural History of Religion.* Oxford: Oxford University Press, 2009.

Iacono, M. *Le fétichisme. Histoire d'un concept.* Paris: Puf, 1992.

Imam Ibn Kathir. *Stories of the Prophets.* Translated and edited by Sheikh Muhammad Mustafa Gemeiah. Mansoura: El Nour, N. D.

Jakobson, Roman. "On Linguistic Aspects of Translation." In *The Translation Studies Reader,* edited by Lawrence Venuti, 126–31. London-New York: Routledge, 2012.

John of Hildesheim. *Historia trium regum.* In F. Schaer, *The Three Kings of Cologne Edited from London.* Lambeth Palace MS 491 (Middle English Texts, 31). Heidelberg: 2000.

Josephus. *The Works of Flavius Josephus.* Translated by William Whiston and A.M. Auburn. Buffalo: John E. Beardsley, 1895. http://data.perseus.org/citations/urn:cts:greekLit:tlg0526.tlg003.perseus-eng1:1.1.

Jung, Carl Gustav. "European Commentary." In Richard Wilhelm, *The Secret of the Golden Flower.* London: Kegan Paul, Trench, Trubner & Co., 1931.

Kirsch, J. *God Against the Gods.* London: Viking Compass, 2004.

Klotz, A. "Sigillaria." In *Realencyclopädie der classischen Altertumswissenschaft,* vol. II A/2, coll. 2278. Berlin-Heidelberg: Springer-Verlag, 1992.

Kohara, Katsuhiro. "Discourses and Realpolitik on Monotheism and Polytheism." *Journal of the Interdisciplinary Study of Monotheistic Religions* 2 (2006): 1–16.

Lampe, G. W. H. *A Patristic Greek Lexicon.* Oxford: Clarendon Press, 1961.

Lang, B. "Monotheismus." In *Handbuch religionswissenschaftlicher Grundbegriffe,* vol. IV, edited by H. Cancik, B. Gladigow and K.-H. Kohl, 148–65. Stuttgart-Berlin-Köln: Kohlhammer, 1998.

Lanzi, F., and G. Lanzi. *Il presepe e i suoi personaggi.* Milan: Jaca Book, 2007.

Leopardi, Giacomo. *Zibaldone,* vol. II, edited by R. Damiani. Milano: Mondadori, 1997.

Lévi-Strauss, Claude. "Santa Claus Burned as a Heretic." In *We Are All Cannibals: And Other Essays,* 1–18. New York: Columbia University Press, 2017.

Lietzmann, H. "Iustinus der Martyrer." In *Realencyclopädie der classischen Altertumswissenschaft,* vol. X/2, coll. 1332–1337. Berlin-Heidelberg: Springer-Verlag, 1992.

Livy. *The History of Rome: Books III and IV With An English Translation.* Translated by Benjamin Oliver Foster. Cambridge, MA: Harvard

University Press; London, William Heinemann, Ltd., 1922. http://data.perseus.org/citations/urn:cts:latinLit:phi0914.phi0014.perseus-eng1:30.

Luzzatto, Sergio. *Il crocifisso di stato.* Torino: Einaudi, 2011.

MacDonald, N. *Deuteronomy and the Meaning of "Monotheism".* Tübingen: Mohr-Siebeck, 2012.

Marquard, Odo. "In Praise of Polytheism (On Monomythical and Polymythical Thinking)." In *Farewell to Matters of Principle: Philosophical Studies.* Oxford: Oxford University Press, 1989.

Martins do Vale, A.M. *Entre a cruz e o dragão: o padroado português na China no século XVIII.* Lisbon: Fundação Oriente, 2002.

Meyer-Lübke, W. *Romanisches Etymologisches Lexicon.* Heidelberg: Uni-Vlg, 1972.

Michels, A. "Review of K. Latte, *Römische Religionsgeschichte.*" *American Journal of Philology* 83 (1962): 434–44.

Miller, D.L. *The New Polytheism: Rebirth of the Gods and Goddesses.* New York: Harper & Row, 1974.

Minucius Felix. *Octavius.* Translated by Robert Ernest Wallis. In *Anti-Nicene Fathers,* Vol. 4, edited by Philip Schaff. https://en.wikisource.org/wiki/Ante-Nicene_Fathers/Volume_IV/Minucius_Felix/The_Octavius_of_Minucius_Felix.

Mitscherlich, A. *Toleranz. Überprüfung eines Begriffs.* Frankfurt: Suhrkamp, 1974.

Mohrmann, C. "Encore une fois: paganus." In *Études sur le latin des chrétiens,* vol. III, 277–89. Rome: Edizioni di Storia e Letteratura, 1977.

More, H. *An Explanation of the Grand Mystery of Godliness.* London: Flesher & Morden, 1660.

———. *Apocalypsis Apocalypseos, or the Revelation of St. John the Divine Unveiled.* London: J. Martyn and W. Kettilby, 1680.

Neusner, J. and B. Chilton, eds. *Religious Tolerance in World Religions.* West Conshohocken, PA: Templeton Foundation Press, 2008.

Nevling Porter, B., ed. *One God or Many? Concepts of Divinity in the Ancient World.* Chebeague, ME: Casco Bay Assyriological Institute, 2000.

Nietzsche, Friedrich. *The Gay Science.* New York: Vintage Books, 1974.

———. *The Twilight of the Idols and the Anti-Christ.* New York: Penguin Classics: 1990.

North, J. A. "Religious Toleration in the Roman Republic." *Proceedings of the Cambridge Philological Society* 205 (1979): 85–103.

Orr, D. G. "Roman Domestic Religion." In *Aufstieg und Niedergang der römischen Welt,* vol. XVI/2, 1563–1578. Berlin-New York: de Gruyter, 1978.

Paper, J. *The Deities Are Many: A Polytheistic Theology.* Albany: State University of New York Press, 2005.

Paschoud, F. "L'intolleranza cristiana vista dai pagani." In *L'intolleranza dei cristiani nei confronti dei pagani,* edited by P. F. Beatrice, 151–88. Bologna: Centro editoriale dehoniano, 1990.

Pater, Walter. *Imaginary Portraits.* Cambridge, UK: Modern Humanities Research Association, 2014.

Perfigli, Micol. *Indigitamenta: divinità funzionali e funzionalità divina nella religione romana.* Pisa: Ets, 2004.

———. "Politeismo." In *Con i Romani*, edited by M. Bettini and W. M. Short. Bologna: Il Mulino, 2014.

Pessoa, F. *Il ritorno degli dèi. Opere di António Mora.* Macerata: Quodlibet, 2005.

Petronius Arbiter. *Satyricon*, edited by Michael Heseltine. London: William Heinemann, 1913. http://data.perseus.org/citations/urn:cts:latinLit:phi0972.phi001.perseus-eng1:29.

Philo. *On the Life of Moses.* http://www.earlyjewishwritings.com/text/philo/book25.html.

Pironti, G. "*Gli dèi e le dèe dei Greci.*" In *L'Antichità. Grecia*, edited by Umberto Eco. Milan: EM Publishers, 2012.

Pörsken, G., and U. Pörsken. "Die Geburt des Helden in Mittelhochdeutschen Epen und Epischen Stoffen des Mittelalters." *Euphorion* 74 (1980): 257–88.

Pound, Ezra. *Guide to Kulchur.* New York: New Directions Books, 1970.

Propp, W. H. C. "Exodus 19–40." In *The Anchor Bible.* New York: Doubleday, 2006.

Puech, A. *Histoire de la littérature grecque chrétienne.* Paris: Les Belles Lettres, 1928.

Purchas, S. *His Pilgrimage, Or Relations of the World and the Religions Observed in All Ages and Places Discovered, from the Creation unto this Present.* London: William Stansby, 1614.

Rank, Otto. *The Myth of the Birth of the Hero: A Psychological Exploration of Myth.* Baltimore: Johns Hopkins University Press, 2004.

Ribbeck, O. *Scaenicae Romanorum poesis fragmenta,* vol. II, *Comicorum fragmenta.* Leipzig: Teubner, 1873.

Rubel, P.G., and A. Rosman, eds. *Translating Cultures. Perspectives on Translation and Anthropology.* Oxford: Berg, 2003.

Rüpke, Jöorg. *The Religion of the Romans.* Cambridge, UK: Polity Press, 2007.

Sabbatucci, D. *Monoteismo.* Roma: Bulzoni, 2001.

Saddington, D.B. "Roman Soldiers, Local Gods and Interpretatio Romana in Roman Germany." *Acta Classica* 42 (1999): 155–69.

Scaliger, Joseph Justus. "Diatriba de Europaeorum linguis." In *Opuscula varia antehac non edita.* Parisiis apud Hieronymum Drouart, 1610.

———. *Prima Scaligeriana, Nusquam antehac Edita.* Utrecht: Peter Elzevir, 1670. Translation by Eva M. Sanford, *Classical Journal* 26, no. 4 (January 1931).

Scheid, John. *Les dieux, l'État et l'individu.* Paris: Seuil, 2013.

———. "Les temples de l'Altbachtal à Trêves: un 'sanctuaire national?'" *Cahiers du Centre Gustave Glotz* 6 (1995): 227–43.

———. "Numa et Jupiter ou les dieux citoyens de Rome." *Archives des Sciences Sociales des Religions* 59, no. 1 (1985): 41–53.

———. "Politique et religion dans la Rome antique. Quelle place pour la liberté de culte dans une religion d'État?" *La Vie des Idées,* June 28, 2011. http://www.laviedesidees.fr/Politique-et-religion-dans-la-Rome.html.

Schmidt, F. "Les polythéismes. Dégénérescence ou Progrès?" In *L'impensable polythéisme. Études d'historiographie religieuse,* edited by F. Schmidt, 13–91. Paris: Éditions des Archives contemporaines, 1988.

Schreiner, K. "Toleranz." In *Geschichtliche Grundbegriffe. Historisches Lexikon zur politisch-sozialen Sprache in Deutschland,* vol. VI, edited by O. Brunner, W. Conze, and R. Koselleck, 445–605. Stuttgart: Klett-Cotta, 1990.

Settis, S. "Severo Alessandro e i suoi Lari." *Athenaeum* 50 (1972): 237–51.

Severi, C. "Autorités sans auteurs: formes de l'autorité dans les traditions orales." In *De l'autorité. Colloque annuel du Collège de France,* edited by A. Compagnon, 93–123. Paris: Odile Jacob, 2008.

Short, W.M. "Metaphor." In *The World Through Roman Eyes,* edited by M. Bettini and W.M. Short. Cambridge, UK: Cambridge University Press, 2018.

Soler, J. "La déesse Syrienne, 'dea peregrina': la mise en récit de l'altérité religieuse dans les 'Métamorphoses' d'Apulée." In *Les représentations des dieux des autres. Actes du Colloque FIGVRA, Toulouse, 9–11 décembre 2010,* edited by C. Bonnet, A. Declerq, and I. Slododzianek, 17–30. Siracusa: Sciascia, 2010.

Stroumsa, G.G. *La formazione dell'identità cristiana.* Brescia: Morcelliana, 1999.

Suetonius. *The Lives of the Twelve Caesars.* Edited by J. Eugene Reed and Alexander Thomson. Philadelphia: Gebbie & Co, 1889. http://data.perseus.org/citations/urn:cts:latinLit:phi1348.abo012.perseus-eng1:7

Tabucchi, Antonio. "Elogio della letteratura." In *Di tutto resta un poco,* 11–19. Milan: Feltrinelli, 2013.

Tacitus. *Germany and its Tribes.* In *Complete Works of Tacitus,* edited by Alfred John Church, William Jackson Brodribb, and Lisa Cerrato. New York: Random House, 1942. http://data.perseus.org/citations/urn:cts:latinLit:phi1351.phi002.perseus-eng1:43.

Tertullian. *Ad Scapulam.* Translated by David Dalrymple. Edinburgh: Murray & Cochrane, 1790. http://www.tertullian.org/articles/dalrymple_scapula.htm.

———. *Apologeticus,* Translated by Alexander Souter. http://www.tertullian.org/articles/mayor_apologeticum/mayor_apologeticum_07translation.htm.

———. *The Prescription Against Heretics.* Translated by Peter Holmes. https://carm.org/tertullian-against-heretics.

Tram Tan Tinh. "Lares." In *Lexicon iconographicum mythologiae classicae,* vol. VI/1, 205–236. Zürich-München: Artemis, 1992.

Van Doren, M. "Peregrina sacra. Offizielle Kultübertragungen im alten Rom." *Historia* 3 (1954): 488–97.

Vermes, G. *The Nativity: History and Legend.* London: Penguin Books, 2007.

Vernant, Jean-Pierre. *Mito e religione in Grecia antica.* Roma: Donzelli, 2009. Translation of *Mythe et Religion en Grèce ancienne.* Paris: Seuil, 1990.

Versnel, H. "Three Greek Experiments in Oneness." In *One God or Many? Concepts of Divinity in the Ancient World,* edited by B. Nevling Porter, 79–164. Chebeague, ME: Casco Bay Assyriological Institute, 2000.

Voltaire. *Treatise on Toleration.* New York: Penguin Classics, 2017.

von Harnack, A. *Lehrbuch der Dogmengeschichte.* Tübingen: Mohr-Siebeck, 1920.

Weissenborn, W. *Ab urbe condita.* Berlin: Weidmannsche Buchhandlung, 1875.

Wissowa, G. "Compitalia." In *Realencyclopädie der classischen Altertumswissenschaft,* vol. IV, coll. 791–792. Berlin-Heidelberg: Springer-Verlag, 1992.

———. *Religion und Kultus der Römer.* Munich: Beck, 1971.

Zagorin, P. *How the Idea of Religious Toleration Came to the West.* Princeton, NJ: Princeton University Press, 2003.

———. "Religious Toleration." In *The Oxford Handbook of the History of Political Philosophy,* edited by G. Klosko, 689–703. Oxford: Oxford University Press, 2011.

Founded in 1893,
UNIVERSITY OF CALIFORNIA PRESS
publishes bold, progressive books and journals on topics in the arts, humanities, social sciences, and natural sciences—with a focus on social justice issues—that inspire thought and action among readers worldwide.

The UC PRESS FOUNDATION
raises funds to uphold the press's vital role as an independent, nonprofit publisher, and receives philanthropic support from a wide range of individuals and institutions—and from committed readers like you. To learn more, visit ucpress.edu/supportus.